The Conscience of a Nation

The Conscience of a Nation

James T. Draper, Jr.

BROADMAN PRESS
Nashville, Tennessee

© Copyright 1983 • Broadman Press
All rights reserved.
4215-30
ISBN: 0-8054-1530-0
Dewey Decimal Classification: 224.8
Subject Heading: BIBLE. O.T. AMOS
Library of Congress Catalog Card Number: 82-073420
Printed in the United States of America

To the churches of the Southern Baptist Convention whose faithfulness to the Lord Jesus Christ first brought me to Him and trained and equipped me for the ministry

Contents

1. **The Conscience of a Nation**
   (Amos 1:1)   9
2. **The Response of a Nation**
   (Amos 1:2—2:3)   21
3. **The Peril of Privilege**
   (Amos 2:4-8)   29
4. **Rejecting God's Provision**
   (Amos 2:9-16)   41
5. **The Voice of the Lord**
   (Amos 3:1-8)   51
6. **The Results of God's Judgment**
   (Amos 3:9-15)   63
7. **Corruption and Ecclesiasticism**
   (Amos 4:1-5)   75
8. **Divine Warnings in Nature**
   (Amos 4:6-13)   85
9. **Repentance or Disaster**
   (Amos 5:1-11)   93
10. **The Fruit of Repentance**
    (Amos 5:12-15)   103

11. **The Dark "Day of the Lord"**
   (Amos 5:16-20)   111
12. **Vain Worship**
   (Amos 5:21-27)   117
13. **The Lap of Luxury**
   (Amos 6:1-6)   123
14. **Impending Judgment**
   (Amos 6:7-14)   129
15. **Trying God's Patience**
   (Amos 7:1-9)   135
16. **Religious Opposition to the Truth**
   (Amos 7:10-17)   141
17. **A Basket of Summer Fruit**
   (Amos 8:1-3)   151
18. **Imminent Judgment**
   (Amos 8:4-14)   163
19. **Inescapable Judgment**
   (Amos 9:1-10)   175
20. **God's Restoration**
   (Amos 9:11-15)   183

1
The Conscience of a Nation
(Amos 1:1)

Amos is one of the most relevant, practical, and contemporary studies found in the Scriptures. The times in which Amos lived are remarkably similar to ours. The difficulties faced and the social and cultural conditions are strikingly like those today. Of all the prophets, none is more apropos for us.

Amos preached in the eighth century BC, delivering his message somewhere around 760 or 750 BC. His contemporaries were Hosea, Isaiah, and Micah.

Amos hailed from the little town of Tekoa, ten miles south of Jerusalem on the edge of the desert. It was hard to make a living in Tekoa. The land was barren and the soil unproductive. Standing on the barren desert land, Amos could view Mount Nebo where Moses died. He could look down the slopes into the Dead Sea. We could not imagine a more desolate place than Amos's hometown.

Amos 7:14 identifies him as a herdsman and a dresser of sycamore trees. The sycamore tree had a fig-like fruit that Amos picked for a living. Sycamore fruit was not especially good. Only really poor people ate it.

Wild beasts preyed upon the sheep, and Amos constantly had to protect them. He had to be diligent in order to make a living.

While tending his sheep and dressing the trees, he became aware of the conditions of his day because he lived on a much-traveled route. Caravans from one side of the land would pass to the other through Tekoa.

At this time, life was extremely difficult for Judah and Israel. Civil war had split them into two divisions, the north and the south. The southern kingdom was Judah and the northern kingdom, Israel. Judah's king was Uzziah, and Israel's was Jeroboam II. During such a time Amos preached. In this period of history, Egypt and Assyria were always vying for world supremacy, perhaps similar to America and Russia today. When one became strong, it attacked the other, passing through Judah and Israel. It was as though Judah and Israel were highways for the conquering armies from the south and the north. The tyranny and sin of Egypt and Assyria hung like ominous shrouds over Judah and Israel.

Around the middle of the eighth century BC, when Amos came to preach, there was a lull in the fighting. Remember, Amos was from Judah in the south, and God called him to go to Israel in the north. That didn't go over very well with Israel. That was like a "rebel" going north and telling a "Yankee" what to do.

In Israel matters were going rather well. There was a period of peace and prosperity between the conquering armies of Assyria and Egypt. Wealth abounded. People lived in luxury and self-indulgence, or they lived in abject poverty. The judiciary was dishonest; government was corrupt. There was evidence everywhere of extortion, riots, violence, and class hatred. Wealth was gained by injustice and oppression. Dishonesty was the rule and not the exception; there was an indifference to suffering. The people who had it good lorded it over those who didn't. They multiplied peace and prosperity into selfishness and self-indulgence.

Religious conditions followed the same pattern. Outwardly religion thrived in Israel. Attendance soared, treasuries bulged with money, and religious pilgrimages to Bethel, Gilgal, and Beersheba were common. Inwardly, there was sickness. The priests were little more than professional leeches. Immorality was practiced in the name of Jehovah. Real righteousness was hated and opposed. There was much insincerity, hypocrisy, and superstition. The people were utterly lacking in an understanding of real religion. There were gross immorality, drunkenness, revelry, and everything that is associated with evil.

Here, it becomes painfully revelant for us today. In this period of relative peace, instead of being grateful to God for the peace and prosperity that he had given, the people used this time to go more deeply into sin. Can't you see the parallel? In spite of current recession, we in America have been living in a time of unprecedented prosperity. There has never been a time when we have had more possessions, more ease, and more evidence of God's blessings materially and socially upon our land. Yet, rather than using these prosperous conditions that God has allowed in our praise and worship of him, we, too, just like Israel, have used prosperity as an occasion to go deeper into sin than ever before. While religion flourishes, real worship of God diminishes. While outwardly it seems that everything is going strong, inwardly there is decay, rottenness, and evil of every kind.

But Amos wasn't deceived by the publicity and outward signs. He saw the judgment of God coming upon the nation. The nation that rebels against God must pay the consequences. If we carefully read the Book of Amos, we will discover that his preaching was sheer desperation. In desperation, he warned the people of impending judgment. And he was right. Within thirty years, Sargon II of Assyria swept into Israel. The Northern Kingdom fell, and the people were scattered in captivity and bondage.

At Bethel, one of the shrines in Israel, was a priest named Amaziah. Amaziah told Jeroboam II that Amos had conspired against him and the house of Israel and that the land was not able to bear all his words (7:10). What had Amos done? He had told the simple truth! Amaziah, the priest who ought to have agreed, said, "The people cannot bear his words." Amos had told them that Jeroboam would die by the sword, and Israel would be led away captive out of their own land. Amaziah ordered Amos to go back where he had come from to prophesy. Amos was delivering God's message, and the priest accused him of prophesying against the king.

The greatest threat to the message of God lies within the religious community! Amos was God's gift to Israel, a rebellious people. He was God's attempt to convey the message to the people. He was the conscience God gave them. Their consciences had been seared. They cared not for the things of God, but Amos was God's special messenger to the people.

In New Testament times, God named pastors, teachers, and evangelists as gifts to the church. God has always had special gifts in the form of people for the church. Amos was God's gift to Israel, yet his greatest opposition came from the religious community.

The fiercest opposition to the cause of Christ today does not lie with Madalyn Murray O'Hair; it lies with the godless consciences of religious leadership. Every major assault in our century upon the church and the Word of God has come through the religious community. God has raised a conscience for his people and for America. It is the message God would deliver through his ministers across the land.

The conscience of a nation is based upon the authority of God's Word. Notice what Amos said about himself: "The words of Amos, . . . which he saw concerning Israel" (Amos 1:1). The word translated "saw" is a most specific Hebrew word. There is a Hebrew word meaning "to see" that implies seeing with the natural eye. It means to look at something with the physical eye and see color, shape, form, beauty, and so forth. But this Hebrew word is one which means to see with the eyes of the Spirit and of spiritual understanding. It signifies seeing something that cannot be seen unless God reveals it. The beginning of this message which Amos delivered to Israel is a reminder that God had revealed to him spiritual truths that had to be declared. Spiritual comprehension can come only through the Spirit.

The conscience of a nation does not speak of social conditions separate from God and his nature, but rather declares, "Thus saith the Lord" (1:3). Notice how this concept is repeated in 7:1,3-9 and 17. God's method of revealing his will is through inspired men who stand upon the authority of God's Word. The prophet has to speak and preach. He has no alternative. There is a divine compulsion about it. He must proclaim, "Thus saith the Lord."

We can debate theology all we want, but the beginning of a valid message from God is based on the authority of the Word of God. We must start with an authoritative Word from God. That is why there is virtually no conscience today. The Word of God is not sufficiently magnified. There are many churches across America which do not preach from the Bible. No wonder there is no conscience in America today! We can dispute what preachers say, but not what God says. The message for the conscience of a nation is based on the authority of God's Word.

The second characteristic of the conscience of a nation is: It is based on the nature of God's character. God is primarily a moral being. Amos accepted that truth and preached it with throbbing intensity. His soul was swept up by it. God is a moral being and all nations are responsible to him. If we can avoid gaining a concept of the character of God, then we can live like we want. We can fuss, fight, disagree, and have everything in our lives that is ungodly and against the purposes of God. But if we once understand the moral nature of God, we cannot live ungodly lives. The conscience of a nation delivers a message that is based on the nature of God's character.

There are four characteristics of God in the Book of Amos we must catch if we are to understand the message as it was delivered. *First is the holiness of God:* "The Lord God has sworn by his holiness that the time will come when he will put hooks in your noses and lead you away like the cattle you are; they will drag the last of you away with fishhooks!" (4:2, TLB). His message of warning, approaching judgment, and retribution was based squarely upon God's holiness. The holiness of God means that God is a complete being. There is no fracturing of God. He is a whole person.

Not only is he whole and complete, but God is different from us. Holiness means he is separate from us, not like us. We are sinful—God is holy. God's holiness needs to be proclaimed. His holiness includes his love and grace. Because he is holy, he moves to provide that which we cannot provide. "He who knew no sin became sin for us that we might be made the righteousness of God" (2 Cor. 5:21). We cannot be holy. Our very best is as filthy rags in his sight. But God, in his holiness requiring perfection of us, moved in his grace to provide that perfection through his Son. The message of God is predicated on the holiness of God.

The second characteristic of God is that of righteousness: "O evil men, you make 'justice' a bitter pill for the poor and oppressed. 'Righteousness' and 'fair play' are meaningless fictions to you!" (5:7, TLB). The easiest way to define "righteousness" is: It is that which is straight as opposed to that which is crooked, that which is perfect as opposed to that which is imperfect, that which is pure as opposed to that which is impure. The righteousness of God implies that God's actions and relationships are always right. He is always straight. There is no perverseness.

James wrote that there is "no variableness, neither shadow of turning" in him (James 1:17). His righteousness is consistent. That will either bring blessing to us or condemnation, depending upon our attitude toward God. If we are right with God, it will be a blessing. If we are walking in harmony with his purposes for our lives, it is wonderful to know that God is righteous. We don't have to wonder how he will respond to any situation. His character is straight. He will always do that which is right.

The third characteristic of God we must understand is the judgment of God. "Ye who turn judgment to wormwood" (5:7). The word *judgment* is translated *justice* in *The Living Bible.* It refers to the decisions of God. God is always going to make the just decision.

People become upset over those who have never heard the gospel. God is a just God. His decisions are always right. No one is "sent to hell." Every man has the opportunity to respond. God sees to that. No one can ever say to God, "You sent me to hell." His justice rests upon his righteousness, and his righteousness rests upon his holiness. We can count on his justice. "Be not deceived," Paul wrote to the churches in Galatia, "God is not mocked: for whatsoever a man soweth, that shall he also reap" (Gal. 6:7). Amos had a very graphic way of putting it. Remember, he was a country boy. In speaking of the judgment of God he observed, "As if a man did flee from a lion, and a bear met him; or went into the house, and leaned his hand on the wall, and a serpent bit him" (5:19). Amos was saying that God's judgment will prevail; you will be found out. We can do as we please, but we must know that God's judgment is irrevocable; it is true, and we will face judgment. The conscience of a nation is based on the justice or judgment of God.

The fourth characteristic is that of grace. "It may be that the Lord God of hosts will be gracious unto the remnant of Joseph" (Amos 5:15*b*). In the midst of thundering judgment, there stands the thrilling call of God's grace. God desires to meet the needs of his people. Every warning God gives us is because he loves us. Amos went into minute detail about how God gives warning:

"I sent you hunger" says the Lord, "but it did no good; you still would not return to me. I ruined your crops by holding back the rain three months before the harvest. I sent rain on one city, but not another. While rain fell on one field, another was dry and withered. People from two or three cities would make their weary journey for a drink of water to a city that had rain, but there wasn't ever enough. Yet, you wouldn't return to me," says the Lord.

"I sent blight and mildew on your farms and your vineyards; the

locusts ate your figs and olive trees. And still you wouldn't return to me," says the Lord. "I sent you plagues like those of Egypt long ago. I killed your lads in war and drove away your horses. The stench of death was terrible to smell. And yet you refused to come. I destroyed some of your cities, as I did Sodom and Gomorrah; those left are like half-burned firebrands snatched away from the fire. And still you won't return to me," says the Lord (Amos 4:6-9, TLB).

Every natural disaster you can imagine is a warning from God because God loves us. I am not claiming that he sits down and plots where to send the next tornado. But I know this: every tornado and every hurricane he allows is a warning from him because he loves us. It is his grace.

Notice what else he had done for them. "I cleared the land of the Amorites before them—the Amorites, as tall as cedar trees, and strong as oaks! But I lopped off their fruit and cut their roots" (2:9, TLB). He rebuked their enemies. He made Israel strong and broke the backs of her enemies, yet they didn't return to him. "I brought you out from Egypt and led you through the desert forty years, to possess the land of the Amorites. And I chose your sons to be Nazirites and prophets" (2:10-11, TLB). He provided miraculously for them and sent them spiritual ministers, all because he wanted them to return to him. We must understand how much God cares about us. He has gone to every imaginable length to draw us to himself.

So, the conscience of a nation is based upon the nature of God's character.

Thirdly, it is based on the requirements of God's holiness. There are only two responses that will keep God's judgment from falling upon us as individuals and as a nation. First is repentance. "The Lord says to the people of Israel, 'Seek me—and live'" (5:4, TLB). "Seek the Lord and live" (5:6, TLB). The word *seek* means to feel out with the hands. It is the picture of a blind person who cannot see, and he feels with his hands or his feet and creates a path in a certain direction. It is also the picture of a person who is lame, blind, and helpless because of his sin and is desperately seeking help. That is the word used here. It speaks of genuine repentance. The only way to God is repentance. As long as we are self-satisfied and condemn others without ever looking at our own lives, we cannot come to God. The requirements of God's holiness are repentance and then obedience.

"For many and great are your sins. I know them all so well . . . Be good, flee evil—and live! . . . Hate evil and love the good" (5:12,14-15, TLB). In other words, obey God. It doesn't do any good to say "Amen" to divine truth if we aren't living it. The conscience of a nation is the people of God who proclaim, "Thus says the Lord: repent and obey."

In the first chapter Amos wrote about the sins of their enemies. Amaziah didn't get too upset with Amos when he preached about the sins of Assyria, Damascus, Gaza, and Egypt. But when Amos got through talking about all those nations, he came back to assert, "Israel knows better. Israel has light. Israel has been chosen by God. Her judgment will be more terrible than the judgment of the pagans."

Jesus gave the same truth when he talked about pagan cities. "Woe to you, Chorazin, and woe to you, Bethsaida! For if the miracles I did in your streets had been done in wicked Tyre and Sidon their people would have repented long ago in shame and humility. Truly, Tyre and Sidon will be better off on the Judgment Day than you! And Capernaum, though highly honored, shall go down to hell! For if the marvelous miracles I did in you had been done in Sodom, it would still be here today. Truly, Sodom will be better off at the Judgment Day than you!" (Matt. 11:21-24, TLB).

Jesus taught that a nation which has a message from God is held accountable for that message. That means it would be better for us to be natives in the darkest corner of the earth, who have never heard the name of Jesus, than to come week after week into the house of God, hear the message, and do nothing about what God calls us to do. The judgment of God will be more severe upon us than many others. That is a staggering principle for us today.

If we regard the tremendous light we possess, our judgment will be more terrible than that on Sodom and Gomorrah. They would have repented if they had seen what we have seen. When we go overseas into lands that haven't heard the message of Christ, people by the thousands flock to Christ. They will walk all night—hundreds of miles—stand endlessly for hours, crying for more. Thousands will be saved. But here in America, we have more important things to do. Twelve o'clock is the magic hour. We think we must leave church right at 12:00 and rush back to all of our other concerns. It will be a sad, sad day when God's judgment ultimately falls upon this land and upon our lives. It is a national truth we must keep in mind.

Finally, it is based upon the desire of God's love.

"Then, at that time, I will rebuild the City of David, which is now lying in ruins, and return it to its former glory, and Israel will possess what is left of Edom, and of all the nations that belong to me." For so the Lord, who plans all, has said, "The time will come when there will be such abundance of crops, that the harvest time will scarcely end before the farmer starts again to sow another crop, and the terraces of grapes upon the hills of Israel will drip sweet wine! I will restore the fortunes of my people Israel, and they shall rebuild their ruined cities, and live in them again, and they shall plant vineyards and gardens and eat their crops and drink their wine. I will firmly plant them there upon the land that I have given them; they shall not be pulled up again," says the Lord your God (9:11-15, TLB).

The desire of God's love is to heal, to save and to forgive. And the conscience of America is a conscience based on the authority of the Word of God, upon the nature of the character of God, and upon the requirements of the holiness of God. But we always have the message of the desire of the love of God for us. It is vitally relevant to our lives. We can start at the place where Amos sought to draw the people.

Do we stand in a relationship approved and accepted by God? Have we been obedient to him? Have we done what God has called us to do? Amaziah was a priest in Israel, but he knew not God!

2
The Response of a Nation
(Amos 1:2—2:3)

Amos was a master preacher—and psychologist. He first spoke about the sins of Damascus, Tyre, Edom, Ammon, and Moab. The Israelites were elated because he was laying it on their enemies. But wait. Soon Amos was coming home with this message: "These nations are responsible, but you're more responsible because you have more light. You have God's Word, God's message, God's prophet. You have been chosen by God. You have the tables of the law which God has given you; you have the sacrificial system and the worship of Jehovah which has been implanted in you. You are more responsible than those nations."

Review the pagan nations Amos identified according to their sins. From his condemnations of each nation, there are truths for us to grasp. These were nations under judgment. God had made them morally responsible to him, and this truth applies no less today. Godless nations are responsible to an almighty, sovereign, moral God. This is an eternal verity. These pagan nations did not have the law written on tablets of stone, but they did have it written in their consciences. God made it manifestly clear that the pagans, though not privileged to have messages from God as did Israel and Judah, were responsible to God.

There are four ideas I want you to consider concerning judgment upon those nations. First of all, notice the Sovereign. Look at God. You cannot fathom what is happening in the Book of Amos until you have looked at God himself. You see, if you do

21

not have the right view of God, you have knotty problems.

Quite frankly that's the root of America's problems today. We have no concept of an eternal, sovereign, authoritative God; we have no idea of a God to whom we are morally responsible. Our idea of God often assumes that he is either an eternal killjoy or a doting, old grandfather—but not one to whom we are personally responsible. So we ignore him, turn away from him, mock him, or laugh at him. We do not give ourselves to him because we really do not understand who he is. We must first be confronted with the Sovereign himself—God.

Notice three truths about the Sovereign. First, *his judgment* is vividly treated at the outset. In verse 2 Amos wrote, "The Lord will roar from Zion." The word *roar* is a vicious, savage word—not an easy word. Amos referred to a lion's roar before he pounces upon his victim, a roar which strikes terror into the heart of its prey. This phrase speaks of imminent danger, destruction, pain, and even impending death. Roar is a word which Amos used in reference to none other than God.

In Judges 14:5, for instance, where Samson is about to kill a lion, the text reads that the lion "roared against him." We could translate it: "The lion attacked him," because Samson turned the lion "every which way but loose." Nevertheless, the lion had designs on Samson. *Roared*. That's the same word used in Amos.

Can we describe God in terms like that? Do we dare believe that our God is One who roars in judgment? A God who roars and warns of impending doom and destruction? Before we can begin to understand the Book of Amos, we must first gaze at God.

Now, God didn't make a hasty judgment. Read through all of the six condemnations. They have a most consistent pattern. Verse 3: "For three transgressions of Damascus, and for four." Verse 6: "For three transgressions of Gaza, and for four." Verse 9: "For three transgressions of Tyrus (Tyre), and for four." Verse 11: "For three transgressions of Edom, and for four." Verse 13: "For three transgressions of the children of Ammon, and for four." Then, in Amos 2:1: "For three transgressions of Moab, and for four."

Here is an unusual pattern. What does it mean? God was indicating, "I was very patient, the first transgression." The first rebellion deserved God's immediate response, but he was longsuffering. The second certainly should have been judged immediately, but God still waited. Though he had raised his fist to strike, God stopped in midair. But when the fourth transgression was committed, God's patience wore thin. God's decision to send judgment was not hasty, but mankind's sin had reached its fullest proportion, and God has to act in judgment.

"The Lord roared," wrote Amos. We must understand a cardinal truth about the Almighty—there is a point beyond which God will not let us go. "My Spirit shall not always strive with man," God warned in the very first book of the Bible (Gen. 6:3).

In the New Testament there are two basic doctrines which express this truth. There is the unpardonable sin: When the wickedness and rebellion of a lost person reaches such proportions that he rejects (and even curses) God as though he were actually Satan (Cf. Matt. 12:22-32). God can reach a point beyond which even he will not go.

Second, if a child of God ever becomes so rebellious and hostile against the purposes of God, God can move in judgment on the life of that Christian. First John 5:16 speaks of "a sin unto death" which is committed by a believer. The Christian guilty of such a sin is called away by the Lord. In this life, judgment falls on disobedient, rebellious believers. Though God is patient and waits in mercy to forgive and forbear, there is a time when "the Lord will roar from Zion," and in judgment God will move upon the people.

Those pagan nations had sinned and overflowed their sin cups; they were running over with rebellion and God said, "I've had enough." And judgment fell like the blade of a guillotine.

Notice not only God's judgment but *his perception*. God sees all—nothing escapes his eyes. Our earthly relationships have a heavenly dimension. What we do toward one another affects our relationship with God. All of the sins mentioned here are those of inhumanity, sins of oppression against another person or persons. Our actions toward mankind provoke reactions from God, and God is protective of everything in our lives.

In the case of Damascus, that city had done unjustly to the Gileadites (v. 3). Hazael's sin was one-half century old. In his case God saw the past—and the sin of Hazael. Even though the sin was past, it was yet an abhorrence to God because it had not been met with the fruits of repentance. God does see unrepentant sins, those sins that might have been forgotten by some. When it came to Gaza, God saw the individual acts of the slave trade, seizing persons and putting them in harness, and selling them as pieces of property or animals (vv. 6-7).

In verse 9, when Amos dealt with Phoenicia or Tyre (Tyrus), he saw that Tyre had made a treaty and broken it. In verse 11, concerning Edom, he saw the hidden hatred, hostility, and bitterness in the hearts of the Edomites. In verse 13 he saw that the emotions and ambitions of Ammon had swallowed up all pity; the Ammonites brutally disregarded the welfare of others as they sought to enlarge their borders.

Going into the second chapter (vv. 1-3), concerning Moab, he saw the memory of cherished sins and bitter hostility which existed in their lives. Amos saw the Sovereign as the Judge because he (Amos) also viewed clearly the heinous sins of those who were to be judged.

Now examine the third thought about the Sovereign: *his requirements*. The essence of these passages is: God still governs nations, and those nations are responsible to him. There is no national sin which goes unnoticed or unpunished. The righteousness of a nation will insure the blessings of God, but its sin will solidify the judgment of God.

Amos let these nations know that no philosophy or ideology can free them or excuse them for trifling with God's requirements. The tidal wave of doom may seem to move slowly, but it moves surely upon those nations who respond in rebellion against God. Amos emphasized the moral responsibility of mankind to God. Many times we wonder about "the heathen," whom we feel have never heard the gospel. We become awfully concerned about them. Amos makes it abundantly plain that they are morally responsible because they have rejected the light God has given them.

In the Book of Amos we are confronted with a God who is a moral being. From this message we should see ourselves and the nations of the world as morally accountable to God. God moved in judgment upon those heathen nations.

I would to God that we could grasp what kind of God we serve. Our concepts of God, for the most part, are so feeble. We must think God has an IQ of 16, and that he has no understanding at all, excusing us for our disobedience and rebellion and for the devious attitudes which impede our service for him. In essence, Amos was preaching, "Listen, you may be living in a nation surrounding Israel and Judah, but you're still responsible to God, even though you don't claim him. God is The God who sees all and knows all. And he is going to move in judgment on you."

Here is a stark reminder to us in America. No nation in the history of the world has enjoyed such sudden prosperity, affluence, and blessing from God as the U.S. God will hold us severely responsible for our reaction to him.

Now, notice the symbol Amos used. First was the Sovereign. Second was the symbol of fire. Throughout this passage Amos used for God and his judgment the symbol of fire. "I will send a fire, I will send a fire, I will send a fire"—over and over again. Hebrews 12:29 states: "Our God is a consuming fire." That is a picture which recurs throughout the Word of God. God was seen in a burning bush. In the fire of that bush God spoke to Moses and called him to service. In Exodus 13 when the people needed protection, there was a pillar of fire by night, which represented the presence, power, and provision of God for their lives. In Exodus 19 the people observed Moses on the mountain as they walked and waited. Smoke boiled from the mountain because God descended on the mountain in fire. In Exodus 24 it is recorded concerning God that "the glory of the Lord was like devouring fire." Fire is a symbol of God and his judgment.

There are several factors about fire which are different from most other elements. First of all, fire is about the most destructive force of all the elements. It destroys; it is a fitting symbol of the destructive power resident in the nature of God. God is a holy God. When his presence enters our lives and meets our sin, it destroys sin. It is a destructive force, but it's also a purifying force. In the ultimate sense it destroys only that which is not valuable. It destroys that which is refuse, wood, hay, and stubble (Cf. 1 Cor. 3:12-13). That which is pure, real, eternal, and zealous, the fire refines. It reveals the character and nature of our Savior. What we desperately need is for the fire of God to destroy that which is an abhorrent to him and destroy that which destroys us. The fire purifies, cleanses, refines, and reveals. It is a symbol of God.

Now notice the self. In Amos 1 and 2 one devilish thread weaves its way. There was among those nations the sin of selfishness, the sin of self-pleasing. They did what they did because they wanted to please themselves. They wanted to get what they wanted. It is a picture of self, proudly trampling on others in order to gain a profit, in order to succeed, in order to gain prosperity. It is a picture of self, and we must see that because your greatest enemy is you. The greatest enemy of me is me. Dear Lord, what you could do with me if it weren't for me—if it weren't for sin and self that always struggle against God. I know God's ways are best, but still I resist. I know God's forgiveness is sweet, but still I fight it. I know God's way is right, but still I debate it within myself. How desperately we ought to reaffirm: "I am crucified with Christ; nevertheless I live; yet not I, but Christ liveth in me; and the life which I now live in the flesh I live by the faith of the Son of God, who loved me, and gave himself for me" (Gal. 2:20). Self, the severest struggle of all, runs like a malignant sore through this passage.

Now rivet your attention on the sin. What sin does he condemn? Bear in mind that here he is speaking to pagan nations—not Israel, not people who had the benefit of prophets, of the written laws, of a privileged system from God. He's speaking to pagan nations, and he describes their sin. Their sin was basically one of cruelty to other people—inhumanity. It was vividly described. In verse 3 concerning the sin of Damascus, the text says that they had "threshed Gilead with threshing instruments of iron." The word *thresh* describes what you do to a grain crop in order to make it profitable. To thresh the grain, you beat it repeatedly. But in threshing you are doing it to things. Hazael and Damascus had done that to people. They had treated people as if they were things, and the judgment of God falls upon those who treat people as if they are mere things.

At Gaza it was slave trade where they traded their fellowman. Tyre signed a treaty giving their word, and they violated it. This passage reveals how much God hates a lie and despises covenant and treaty breaking. And these people violated their treaty and entered into slave trading.

For the Edomites there was bitterness and hatred toward their brothers. This is described in vivid detail in verse 11. In Ammon there was an ambition to be bigger than they were, and to have more land than they possessed. They responded with cruelty, violence, and murder against their brothers in order to seize it (v. 13). Moab had a violent and vindictive hatred, one of attitude and action toward others. And in this passage, you'll find that four times out of the six, God said, "Thus saith the Lord," "because they have" (v. 3); "because they carried" (v. 6); "because they delivered" (v. 9); "because he did pursue" (v. 11); "because they have ripped up the women with child" (v. 13); and "because he burned the bones" (2:1). God had responded because of their horrid actions toward others. God hates inhumanity and oppression of every kind. I wonder what God is going to do in our world? Never in the history of the world has there been such a cold, calculating inhumanity among nations as exists today. In our lifetime there have been atrocities, acts of oppression, sins of violence, movements of inhumanity that nations have perpetrated against one another, and I have to believe that God will respond. God will punish.

Now God's message to those pagan nations is also a stern warning to us. If God held those pagan, heathen nations responsible, we are even more responsible. If God judged them, surely he judges us. If he were patient with them, surely he is patient with us, but there reaches a time when patience can no longer endure. There has to be a forceful moving of God in the experience of his people.

We pray for revival; we talk about it. But, folks, when revival comes, God uses the *fire* of revival, right? I want you to realize that fire is not only revealing, but also destructive and purifying. It tears away that which is surface, that which is hypocritical, that which is shallow, that which is meaningless. I believe with all of my heart that God is going to come in revival during our day. I pray that he'll do it and that he will help us understand what it's going to require of us. We must become honest with him. We must lay our lives before him. There must be perfect obedience to him if he's to have liberty to move in blessing among us.

3
The Peril of Privilege
(Amos 2:4-8)

Here's what happened in Israel; the same thing has happened to us today. Israel had accepted the wonderful fact of God's election. God had chosen Israel as a nation. They were a unique people, a peculiar people; they had a special relationship with God.

They took this idea that they were the chosen people of God and concluded that they were God's pets, that they could get anything they wanted out of God, and that the rules God applied to other people didn't apply to them. They were exceptions to the rules. They could do as they pleased and get by with it, because, after all, they were God's chosen people. They enjoyed an exalted position among the nations.

But God counseled them that, while there were some distinctive characteristics to the nation of Israel, he is a God of unchanging righteousness and judgment; and his righteousness operates just as surely within the family of God as it does without. God was speaking through Amos that the sins of pagan nations were sins also seen among God's people.

The unique position granted to them by God's grace (far from excusing their sins) made their sins more horrible, more treacherous, for they did not understand that the uniqueness which made them God's people also carried with it a unique responsibility and peril. Israel, the chosen nation, was benefited by special teaching, special protection, and special guidance from Jehovah. The nation also had enlightened reason and conscience which God had given to them. They also had a written reservoir of the Word of God—the Law and the words of the prophets, inspired by God.

Yet they rebelled against God, and Amos proclaimed, "Thus saith the Lord": upon you shall fall the full judgment of God because you have sinned against tremendous light. In Luke Jesus concluded a story and said, "To whomsoever much is given, of him shall be much required" (12:48). The person to whom much light is given has great responsibility. That was the setting for Amos's message here:

> Thus saith the Lord; For three transgressions of Judah, and for four, I will not turn away the punishment thereof; because they have despised the law of the Lord, and have not kept his commandments, and their lies caused them to err, after the which their fathers have walked: But I will send a fire upon Judah, and it shall devour the palaces of Jerusalem. Thus saith the Lord; For three transgressions of Israel, and for four, I will not turn away the punishment thereof; because she sold the righteous for silver, and the poor for a pair of shoes; That pant after the dust of the earth on the head of the poor, and turn aside the way of the meek: and a man and his father will go into the same maid, to profane my holy name: And they lay themselves down upon clothes laid to pledge by every altar, and they drink the wine of the condemned in the house of their god (vv. 4-8).

This was a message of prophecy to God's people. It was a warning that there was great peril and great responsibility. This hits us in twentieth-century America. We are extremely privileged; we have great access to the Word of God, to the message of God, to the truth of God, and there is an awesome responsibility which goes with such a privilege.

There are two major thoughts I want you to see in this passage. First, *notice that these privileged people rejected God's truth.* In verses 4 and 5, the message is clear. Judah had rejected the truth of God. We see also in verses 11 and 12 that the sin of rejecting God's truth was also the case in Israel, for in verse 11 the prophet wrote: "I raised up of your sons for prophets, and of your young men for Nazarites. Is it not even thus, O ye children of Israel? saith the Lord. But ye gave the Nazarites wine to drink; and commanded the prophets, saying, Prophesy not." They rejected the truth of God in Israel *and* in Judah. The sin so vehemently condemned here is the transgression of people who have heard the truth of God, who have received it into their minds, but who have rejected it in their lives.

Now, how did that happen? Verse 4 tells us several things about how they rejected the truth of God. First of all, they rejected the truth of God *by preferring the traditions of men.* The life-style to which they committed themselves was the same to which their fathers had clung. They possessed the law of the Lord, but they preferred the traditions of men. Human authority is no safe guide for conduct. Only God's authority is safe and reliable for us to base our lives upon. But these people began to rely upon their own judgment and that of society.

The people had written and preached deposits of the Word of God. In our day, we have written deposits of the completed Scriptures. God has given the canon of the Scriptures to us. The hallmark of God's people has always been their recognition of the divine Word of truth and their determination to use God's Word as a criterion for judgment, thus rejecting the traditions of men. Every problem known to our churches today is because we have preferred the traditions of men to the Word of God. Every problem existing in our homes and in our communities today is because we have preferred the traditions of men to the Word of God.

If we will abide by the Word of God, God will bless it and multiply it. If we obey God, he will make that Word fruitful in our lives. But what do we do? We read where it teaches that we're supposed to do this or that—let's simply use tithing as an example, all right? *I know the Bible says I ought to tithe,* I say to myself, *but I don't see how I can do that. I don't believe I can.* God says you could; God says he'd stretch the nine-tenths more than the ten-tenths, and those who have tried it have found that to be true. But we prefer our own judgment and the traditions of men to the Word of God. Then we wonder why God doesn't bless us. Let's use witnessing as an example. We say, "Surely God didn't mean for everybody to be a soul-winner, for everybody to be a witness." Of course, he did; that's what he teaches in the Bible. But we've made a whole cult over, "Well, some can and some can't, and it's not everybody's responsibility." We have passed man's judgment upon the Word of God.

Or another thought: Some people say, "I don't have to come to church to worship God." Did you ever hear that? Sure you have. Where do you pick that up in the Bible? Show me one place in the Word of God which says you ought to go out on a mountainside and worship God. It's always the house of God, the people of God, the place of God, the sacred place. There has always been a sacred place where God's people acknowledge to the world that they believe in him. I know you can worship outside the house of God and away from the church building, but when you come to the house of worship you're giving a testimony to the world that you've committed your life to God and that you're earnestly seeking to do his will. When you go out to the lake or to a mountain or somewhere else, no one realizes why you're there. To be honest about it, you probably don't do much worshiping when you're baiting a hook. They rejected the truth of God by preferring the traditions of men.

Secondly, they rejected the truth of God by preferring a lie to that truth. God's law and God's truth stand in opposition to lies and untruth. When anything other than the Word of God is given supreme place in your life, then you have accepted a lie instead of the truth. When we accept the truth, it safeguards us from lies and falsehoods. The people of Israel and Judah fell into lies when they strayed from the truth. The best way to avoid lies is to live for the truth. Stand by the truth. Put God's word in your heart and mind. Give yourself to the truth, and the truth will protect and guard you. God's truth will become your safeguard, and you will have life indestructible because you walk in the power of his truth. Jesus emphasized, "Ye shall know the truth, and the truth shall make you free" (John 8:32). But Israel preferred a lie to the truth.

The third fact this verse tells us is that they not only rejected the truth but *they refused to cultivate it.* Notice these words, "they have despised the law." They had not kept his commandments. If you keep something, you nurture it, you cultivate it, you do whatever's necessary to take care of it. They did not keep God's word, so they were led astray. They were not led astray when they rejected the truth of God, but when they refused to cultivate that truth. All these words indicate a cultivation. *Despise* is a word which refers to a mental state whereby someone judges something unworthy and then rejects it. That's the kind of cultivation we put into the truth that destroys its working in our lives. The word *kept* indicates that we have a kind of life that results in a particular conduct. We have not kept his commandments, so we walk in falsehood and lies. If something is a lie, or we judge it to be a lie, then we have to form a mental appraisal of it, and we thus commit ourselves to falsehood. Amos was saying: Once we have rejected the truth, we embrace a lie, and it controls our lives.

When you have judged God's Word to be unworthy, it's going to express itself in how you live. When you abandon fellowship with God, it cannot help but show in how you live. Wrong belief will result in wrong conduct. We often reject the truth because we do not cultivate the truth. You ask, How do you cultivate it? You do it by using what you have, by committing yourself to the truth you do have. You obey God's Word in truth, and as you obey it, you're able to receive more truth. Or I could put it another way. If you live up to the light you have, God gives you more light. It's as simple as that.

Many of us are waiting for God to send us a special-delivery letter from heaven about some *great big* decision, but we refuse to obey him at the point of how we live in our homes, how we discipline ourselves and our Christian conduct, how we worship him in our church and in our homes, and how we study his Word. There have been times when we refused to do all that. But let a crisis come, and we expect God to continue to reveal deep truth to us, even if we are not obedient to the truth we have. When you receive light you are responsible for the light.

In John 21 Jesus was talking with Simon Peter after the resurrection. They apparently were walking the beach together, and it seems as though Simon Peter remarked, "Lord, I'm willing to do what you want me to do, but what about John?" Do you remember the answer Jesus gave Peter? "If I will that he tarry til I come, what is that to thee? follow thou me" (v. 22). In other words, "Simon Peter, that's none of your business; what I have to do with John is between John and me, but you have a responsibility to do what I committed to you." If we will cultivate the truth of God by being obedient to the light he's given us, and submissive to his calling, it will open the door for us to walk in his light and in his fellowship. But when we reject the truth, refuse to cultivate the truth, and adopt lies instead of truth, such an attitude toward God always brings judgment.

In verse 5 Amos said, "I will send a fire upon Judah, and it shall devour the palaces of Jerusalem." The judgment of God must begin at the house of God, and do not think for a moment that we as God's privileged people are going to escape the judgment of God. By the way, don't fall prey to the habit of assuming that America is God's people like Israel was. We are not. I've heard people boast, "We're God's people; God's not going to let anything happen to us."

In the first place, that's based on a faulty premise because Israel was God's people and God let everything happen to Israel. In fact, God sent it. God said, "I'm even going to use a pagan nation to judge you." But do not say, "Well, we're Gods' chosen people." No, we're *privileged*. God has given us a nation where we can hear his Word and receive his truth. God help us not to reject the truth or judgment will come. And the judgment coming across the world upon this nation may well be the hand of God upon his own people.

Can you explain why the nation which has spent more money in foreign aid and relief of suffering humanity is possibly the most-despised nation in the world today? That doesn't make sense, does it? We are finding ourselves succumbing slowly but surely to antipathy and hostility from other nations that is inexplicable to anything in past history. It may well be the judgment of God upon us as a people who should know better, who do know better, but who have rejected the truth.

Second of all, not only did they reject the truth of God, *but they rejected the way of God*. They rejected God's way—then they rejected God's truth. "You've despised my word, you've not kept my commandments, and you've followed lies just like your fathers" (author's paraphrase).

Now in verse 6, he gives some examples. He exposes three sins in the lives of Israel that confirm the charges he has leveled. Before I list them, let me remind you: God's people were guilty of the same atrocities, the same rebellion, and the same rejection as their pagan and lost neighbors. And those pagans didn't have the prophets! Not one of those nations had a prophet of God in them. They didn't have the divine oracles Israel had, yet Israel was responsible unto God for being guilty of the same sins. God help us!

Here are the three sins Amos mentioned. First is the fact that they had become so covetous that materialism had become a way of life. Verses 6 and 7 talk about selling "the righteous for silver and the poor for a pair of shoes: . . . they pant after the dust of the earth on the head of the poor, and turn aside the way of the meek." These people had become so consumed with material lusts that they wanted only the luxuries and diversions of the world. Israel was absolutely beside itself and madly in love with entertainment, recreation, drunkenness, and immorality. The people had sold their souls for material pleasures. Covetousness was their style. They had oppressed the poor. They had robbed those who were less fortunate than they. God said, "How disgusting. Covetousness has become a condoned practice, as a way of life among my own people!"

Then Amos mentioned immorality. He referred to a man and his father going into the same maid, "to profane his holy name." Take notice here. He pointed out their sensual, sexual lust which pervaded their society. We all are aware that's the kind of society we live in today, a sensual society that is sex-sick. This is how it was in Amos's day.

Here's what they were doing: Israelite fathers and sons who claimed to worship Jehovah would go to a pagan temple where there were prostitutes who gave themselves in worship of Baal, which was the worship of the senses, especially lust. Baal was the worship of the physical and material. The word *Baal* was used synonymously in Scripture with a hedonistic attitude of "live for the flesh and its passions." They had actually given themselves to an act of "worship" to satisfy the sensual gratification and lust of the people. Review the statement, "a man and his father will go in unto the same maid, to profane my holy name." They committed fornication, and they profaned the name of God. In other words, they did it to lash out at God! Their immorality was a direct defiance of God.

When we do what we understand to be offensive to God, we do it to offend God. Do you understand what sin is? Sin is not merely a shame; it's not just a misfortune when we who have the truth of God sin. You may not think about it at the time, and you may not understand it completely, but you are doing it to offend him. "Well, I wouldn't do that," you remark. Yes, you do! When you deliberately and knowingly continue in sins that are against the ways of God, you are doing it to offend God himself.

You cannot separate God and his Word. Disregard and reject his Word and you reject God. Those people who claimed Jehovah God would argue they were doing it because it was worship, and those women were servants of Baal, a god. Amos cried, "Hey, you're not worshipers of Baal. You're worshipers of Jehovah, and yet you justify what you're doing based on pagan rules." They did it to profane the name of the living God. If only you and I could understand that every sin is not just something we do to satisfy ourselves, but every sin we commit is an attempt consciously or unconsciously to strike out against God. That makes every sin a terrible atrocity. Every sin is deeply vulgar, grossly evil, exceedingly wicked because it is an affront to God. It is an offense to God; so it was in defiance of God's command.

Of course, the next fact is most logical. When you have made materialism a way of life, and when you have involved yourself in lust and immorality in defiance of God, the next step is for your worship to become meaningless and perverted. And that's exactly what happened. In verse 8, "They lay themselves down upon clothes laid to pledge by every altar, and they drink the wine of the condemned in the house of their God." Now the altar and the house of their God speak of worship where the sacrifices were made. It is the altar on which atonement was made. The altar was the climax of their obedience to God. Yet, they were going through the motions of coming to the altar and to the house of God. They were regular in worship, but when they came to worship they lay down upon clothes "laid to pledge."

That may not seem important to us, but in Old Testament times, if someone owed you something you could take their clothes as collateral for a loan or whatever they owed. Those were days when people did not have all that many of us do today. The cloak was the outer garment which was their protection from the elements. They needed it desperately, if they were to survive. The Old Testament law was that if they took a cloak in pledge, they would have to give it back before sundown. They couldn't keep it overnight; they not only were despising God's law but were rejecting this truth. They had perverted their worship. What a tragedy! There at the altar in the house of God, where traditionally God met man in mercy and forgiveness, they had twisted their worship and had given every evidence of abusing one another. The cloak they kept was a sign of heartless cruelty and the darkest covetousness. They came to the altar of God with brazen evidence of their sin.

You cannot be right with God and wrong with man. Jesus put it another way in Matthew 5 when he taught, "If thou bring thy gift to the altar, and there rememberest that thy brother hath ought against thee; [He didn't say that you have ought against your brother, but your brother has ought against you.] Leave there thy gift before the altar, . . . first be reconciled to thy brother, and then come and offer thy gift." Notice he said, "Leave there thy gift before the altar. He didn't say don't give it until you get right. He said to leave it at the altar. Can you imagine what would happen if people followed that? I can imagine it: Someone comes up to our business administrator, "Brother, here's a check for $1,000. This is my gift for the cause of Christ, but there's a brother who has something against me. You hold that. Don't spend it until I've made it right with my brother, and I'll come tell you that it's OK." Leave the gift, then go get right.

These people came to the altar virtually smelling of their rebellion against God, with bold evidence of their sin. They went through the motions of worship, perverting and polluting the very act of worship. They had rejected God's truth, and thus they rejected God's way. God asserted, "I will not turn away the punishment thereof" (v. 6).

We are privileged people, privileged to have all the understanding about the Word of God ever needed, but with that privilege there is a peril and also a heavy responsibility. You are responsible for the light God has given you. You are responsible for the truth God has placed in your heart. Expand your understanding and enlarge the truth of God in your heart by obeying and acting upon the truth God has revealed to you.

4
Rejecting God's Provision
(Amos 2:9-16)

In a capsule, judgment upon God's people is the essence of the entire Book of Amos. In this passage, we have a contrast between the faithfulness of God and the unfaithfulness of man, a contrast between God's provision for Israel at every point and Israel's rebellion against God, in spite of everything God had done for the nation. This makes the passage doubly relevant for us today. It speaks to our contemporary society in a country that has been so marvelously blessed by the hand of God.

As Amos began this passage of Scripture, he started by reminding them of what God had done. Verse 9 says, "Yet destroyed I the Amorites before them." After he had previously spoken about the injustice, insensitivity, and compromise of Israel, Amos contended that they had sinned in spite of the fact that God destroyed the Amorites, their enemies.

Then he described the strength of the Amorites. It was impossible for Israel to defeat them, yet God destroyed them. "Also I brought you up from the land of Egypt, and led you forty years through the wilderness, to possess the land of the Amorite. And I raised up of your sons for prophets, and of your young men for Nazarites. Is it not even thus, O ye children of Israel? said the Lord. But ye gave the Nazarites wine to drink; and commanded the prophets, saying, 'Prophesy not'" (2:10-12). In other words, what was about to happen to them was coming by his hand.

> *I am pressed under you, as a cart is pressed that is full of sheaves.*
> *Therefore the flight shall perish from the swift, and the strong shall not*
> *strengthen his force, neither shall the mighty deliver himself: Neither*
> *shall the hand that handleth the bow; and he that is swift of foot shall*
> *not deliver himself:* . . . *And he that is courageous among the mighty*
> *shall flee away naked in that day, saith the Lord (2:13-16).*

This passage sets before us two tremendous truths. We see
them running throughout, and they are reminders to us. The
themes are, *You can be sure your sin will find you out* and *God is going*
to be faithful in spite of man's unfaithfulness. Part of the faithfulness
of God is the fact that God is going to keep his word. If his
people don't do what he has called them to do, then he himself
will judge them. God indeed will be the one who brings
chastisement upon us.

The Bible clearly articulates this truth. "For whom the Lord
loveth he chasteneth" (Heb. 12:6). I need to remind you that
you were as close to your daddy when he was spanking you as
when he was hugging you. God will be faithful! God will be true
to his character, to his nature. If his people are unfaithful and
rebellious, if we do not heed his Word, God will judge; and we
will be fighting against God. We cannot win when we fight
against God.

This passage has three basic divisions. Verses 9 and 10 talk to
us about God's redemption and providence. Here is a beautiful
description of what God had done for them:

> *Yet destroyed I the Amorite before them, whose height was like the*
> *height of the cedars, and he was strong as the oaks; yet I destroyed his*
> *fruit from above, and his roots from beneath. Also I brought you up*
> *from the land of Egypt, and led you forty years through the wilderness,*
> *to possess the land of the Amorite. And I raised up of your sons for*
> *prophets and of your young men for Nazarites. Is it not even thus, O ye*
> *children of Israel? saith the Lord (2:9-11).*

The Nazarites set themselves apart by how they wore the
clothes assigned to them, by how they restricted what they ate

and what they did. They became examples of those totally committed to God. So God gave them as a godly example. And he sent the prophets to declare the truth of his heart. But the people rejected all of them.

Before he spoke of the judgment of God, Amos reminded them of the redemptive purposes of God. Notice his words and how they relate to us. "I brought you up out of the land of Egypt" (v. 10). When he brought Israel out of Egypt, he brought slaves out of Egypt. They could not help themselves; they could not free themselves from Pharaoh. They were helplessly bound in slavery, but God had brought them up. Isn't that what happens when we are saved? God reaches down to touch lives which are helplessly, hopelessly lost in trespasses and sins, doomed for an eternal separation from God. God reaches down into the slavery of sin, draws us to his heart, and frees us. God's redemptive purposes are so clearly seen in our lives.

Amos then reminded them that God led them through the wilderness. That is a touching thought to me because the wilderness itself was a result of their rebellion. God had directed them to possess the land, and you will remember that the people came to Kadesh-barnea and sent twelve spies into the land. The spies came back and ten of them warned, "There are too many of them. They are too strong. They are too big. We can't take the cities." Only two of the twelve, Joshua and Caleb, said, "Yes, we can." The majority ruled, and the people turned away and disobeyed God.

Their forty years in the wilderness was a result of rebellion, but God affirmed, "I led you anyway. I provided for you. I guided you. I directed you." I believe that is a reminder that everything God does with us is by grace. Even when we sin, God loves us. All that God does for you and me is designed to draw us to himself. All he does is out of love, and he blesses us and works in our lives, not because we deserve it, but because of his grace which he freely bestows on us.

He reiterated, "I led you forty years through the wilderness," and, "I led you to possess the land of the Amorites." He destroyed the enemy, the Amorites, before them, and they possessed the land. I think of how many times God has touched my life and has destroyed the enemy before me, how often God has moved in power and blessing in my life—as he loved me, forgave me, and drew me to his heart. He reminds them of all he had done. Hasn't he done as much for us? What a joy he is. Think of his redemptive acts for us: when he touched us to save us, to give us forgiveness, removing guilt from our lives and putting us in the position to receive all the blessings of eternity. He's saved us and guided us. He has never left us alone. In the dark valleys he has been the Light that has shone to carry us through. In the lonesome times, he has been the companion who has made it possible for us to stand victorious. Whenever there was famine he was our food. Whenever there was hurt he was our healing. Amos wanted them to remember what God had done for them.

Then he said, "God did more than that. God gave you, from your own children, Nazarites and prophets: those who proclaim the Word of God." Isn't that what God has done for us? God has given us in this land many of godly example—those who stand as the epitome of Christian love and virtue. He has granted us many godly mothers and consecrated fathers. He has "gifted" us with proclaimers of the Word of God—in their hands and hearts to preach, "Thus saith the Lord." And he did that for Israel. God's redemption and provision have been gracious to us. I had a man in my office whose business is getting Bibles behind the Iron Curtain. We talked about how hard it is for those captive peoples to have the Word of God in their languages, how it is not possible for them to purchase and have free access to the Bible. But we do! Is it worse for someone to have the Word of God and ignore it or to desire it and not have it? We have God's Word.

Amos dealt with God's redemption. Then in verse 12, he

moved to mankind's rejection. Oh, how subtle it is! "But ye gave
the Nazarites wine to drink; and commanded the prophets,
saying, Prophesy not" (v. 12). Here is the subtlety of man's
rejection. This is also happening in our day, even as it did then.
The Nazarites had taken a vow unto God that their lives and
their bodies were sacred and holy before God. They would not
defile their bodies with wine or strong drink. But the people
tempted the Nazarites. "Here is wine for you to drink." In other
words, they compromised the Nazarites, trying to rob them of
their virtues, to spoil their reputations, and to turn their
characters from God. The Israelites rejected God by compromising godly people. This is one of the most subtle sins in America
today. Wherever you see an individual—a man, woman, child, or
young person—who is standing for God, there is the subtle
attempt of Satan through our society to compromise that person's
godliness. I have never seen such strong pressure. Satan has
mounted an assault against the home, against the minister,
against the teacher, against the church member. He attacks
anyone who tries to be godly. Part of man's rejection of God is to
compromise a godly individual. There is an all-out movement in
this country among the media to discredit godly men who are
preaching the gospel. Man's rejection of God is channeled
toward the discrediting and compromise of God's servants. It was
just as true then as it is now.

This passage further says, They "commanded the prophets,
saying, Prophesy not." They didn't want to hear the preaching
and we don't want to hear the message of God, either. Many of
us attend church to hear soothing words to make us feel good
about our sins. We hope the preacher will have "itching ears"
and condone our evil. Let me preach on the home. I tell the
husbands that they are to be men who love their wives just like
Jesus loved the church, that they are to be unselfish and self-
sacrificing for them, and that they are not to be dictators, beating
them over the head. What happens?

A wife will say to her husband, "See, I told you to leave me alone. I'm going to do what I want to do, and you leave me alone." They take my preaching as justification for their lack of submission. Then I preach to the wives that they ought to submit to their husbands in all things, and their husbands go home, justifying their unChristian, ungodly, dictatorial attitudes on the basis of what I have preached to the wives. We are always looking at what God says to somebody else to justify our rebellion. That happened in Israel as they said to the prophets, "Don't you preach. Leave us alone. We will do what we want to do. We don't want to hear what God has to say. Don't prophesy."

After grappling with mankind's rejection, Amos showed the inevitable judgment of God that came. God is our greatest hope, but he is also our greatest threat. Adrian Rogers has observed, "I am not nearly as concerned about what Russia may do to us as what God may do to us." In these verses is the declaration of God that "unless my people turn to me there will be judgment," and God always used the judgment of a pagan nation. Don't think for one moment that God will not use atheistic, Communist Russia or Red China to judge America. He could do that. Such is the testimony of history and of the Word of God. Verse 13 says, "I will make you groan" (TLB). It is a picture that Israel would understand. Think of an oxcart, loaded down with grain so heavily that it creaks everytime the wheels move. As it rolls toward the threshing floor, it finally collapses under the load. God said, "I will do the same to you."

He described it: "Therefore the flight shall perish from the swift, and the strong shall not strengthen his force, neither shall the mighty deliver himself: Neither shall he stand that handleth the bow; and he that is swift of foot shall not deliver himself: neither shall he that rideth the horse deliver himself" (vv. 14-15). Here was the problem: Israel's sins were the same as the heathen nations around them, but there was a difference. God had given Israel the truth. God commanded, "This is what you are to do," and Israel replied, "We won't do it. We refuse to do it." The deepest sin possible is to possess the revelation of God and ignore it. The worst situation in which you could find yourself would be to know what God wants you to do and not do it. What a perilous place! "For whom the Lord loveth he chasteneth." God will not let his people get away with sin. He is a "jealous" God of the covenant, and God's covenant with himself means that, even if we are unfaithful in keeping our part, he'll be faithful to his.

When my children were growing up—even if they disobeyed or were unfaithful as children—I was faithful, and I disciplined them. Even though they did not understand it, and didn't like it and didn't want it, I was going to keep my part of the bargain between parent and child. God is going to do the same with us. We can be unfaithful to God, but God is going to be faithful with us. I submit to you that when God judges a nation, there is no hope of staying his hand. You can stop God's hand only one way, and that is repentance.

God told Jonah to preach *against* Nineveh. Notice he did not announce to those folks at Nineveh: "If you would repent, God wouldn't destroy you." All he said was: "God is going to destroy you in forty days." Forty days and it would all be over (see Jonah 3:1-4). He didn't tell them to repent. He didn't tell them God loved them. He told them that God was going to get them! But they repented, and God didn't destroy them. There is only one thing that stays the hand of God upon any people. "One law and one manner shall be before you, and for the stranger that sojourneth with you" (Num. 15:16). If you sin presumptuously and shake your fist in the face of God, you can know that God is going to judge you. God is going to come, and there is no sacrifice for that. The most desperate need for us is to obey the light we have. We desperately need to obey God. Do what he says.

These are critical days. The time for playing church is over.

The day for us to go along in our complacency is past. We don't have that luxury. Repentance is the only hope for our country. In 2 Chronicles 20, the nation was having difficulty, and the Southern Kingdom of Judah was led by Jehoshaphat. Word came that the Moabites and the Ammonites had gathered and marshaled their forces against Judah. Here was what Jehoshaphat did. First of all, he feared (v. 3). Maybe we need to become scared about our nation and world. We think that if only the crime rates will come down, everything will be fine; if only inflation is going to stop its upward spiral; if only Russia is going to be nice and leave us alone, and if only we can go back to our nice way of living and let the rest of the world go, it'll be all right. Maybe we need to be frightened and to see ourselves on a toboggan slide to destruction. That's what happened in Judah.

Jehoshaphat feared, and then he set himself to seek the Lord. He proclaimed a fast. He called Judah together, and "all Judah stood before the Lord, with little ones, their wives, their children (2 Chron. 20:13). The nation stood together, fasting, praying, seeking God." Then God answered and consoled them, "Be not afraid, nor dismayed by reason of this great multitude; for the battle is not yours, but God's. Tomorrow go ye down against them: . . . Ye shall not need to fight in this battle: set yourselves, stand ye still, and see the salvation of the Lord with you . . . tomorrow go out against them: for the Lord will be with you" (2 Chron. 20:15-17). Verse 29 says that the fear of God fell on all those pagan countries when they had heard that the Lord fought against the enemies of Israel. The hope of staying the hand of judgment is a supernatural intervention of God. You can call it revival, renewal, or whatever. It is the mighty moving of God in the lives of his obedient children in this land.

So, Amos reminded them, "Remember what has been done, and yet you reject him. God is coming in judgment." In my heart I know that God is getting ready to judge this land. I am not an alarmist, but I believe in my soul that God is poised. Billy

Graham has observed that if God doesn't judge America, he will have to apologize to Sodom and Gomorrah. I believe that judgment is coming—in a sense, it is already here. In Romans 1, Paul wrote that when God gets fed up, he turns men loose to their own lusts and appetites. That is happening everywhere. The lust of homosexuality, the lust of incest, the lust of immorality, the lust of unbridled greed for wealth and power. There is only one alternative, and that is for people of the Book, the people who have God's Word, to preach and teach and live that Word.

5
The Voice of the Lord
(Amos 3:1-8)

The first eight verses of Amos 3 speak to us specifically about God, God's voice, God's Word, "The Lord hath spoken." Verse 1 goes, "The Lord hath spoken." Later verse 8 says, "The Lord God hath spoken."

Suppose you go home one day and you turn on the television. Maybe you're watching a situation comedy. About halfway through the program, something goes wrong with the audio and the visual; all you hear is that someone interrupts the program for a special announcement, "The next voice you hear will be the voice of God." You would probably do what I would. You'd think, *Oh, come on. You're putting me on.* You'd think it was a hoax.

But suppose it could be proven beyond a shadow of a doubt that the next voice was indeed the voice of God. What would you do? I tell you what I'd do. I'd move out on the edge of my seat, turn the volume up a bit, and turn my head to the side because I'd want to hear every word. I think that you would, too. I believe we would hang breathlessly upon every word God might speak to us.

That would be a dramatic intrusion into our lives, a spectacular way for God to speak to us. But the Bible declares plainly that God has spoken, and the greatest need of our day is to hear the voice of the Lord—and what God has to say. I believe with all of my heart, as the Bible claims for itself from one end to the other, that the Book is indeed God's voice speaking to us. The dreadful tragedy is that we do not listen to the voice of God. How rare to find a person who is quiet enough to listen to the voice of God. We are so mobile—always doing and always going. It seems so difficult for us to stop, to be still long enough to hear the voice of God.

This passage vividly sets before us the word of the Lord, the voice of the Lord. The first two verses we would call *responsibility*, for in a nutshell they remind us that those to whom God has spoken have an urgent responsibility to respond to what God has said. When God does reveal himself to us, and when his voice is heard, we had better respond. We must obey and listen to the voice of God.

Look at several ideas in these verses. "Hear this word that the Lord hath spoken against you" (v. 1). Now the word *against* could be translated "about you." "Here is what God has spoken about you. Hear God's conclusion about you." If there is anything that must happen in your life and mine and in our society, it is for us to hear God's opinion—what God thinks of us. We need to see clearly the condition of our lives, our families, our churches, and our nation from God's standpoint. We don't see things as God does. We have false measurements. We measure by the veneer, by that which is on the surface.

You'll remember when Samuel went to the house of Jesse in Bethlehem to anoint a new king. God had told Jesse to bring all his sons out, and a king would be chosen from among them. Right off the bat, Jesse trotted out his tallest, handsomest, most vigorous, and most talented son named Eliab. When Samuel saw him, you could just read it: there was a sense of "Wow! This is the one." "Surely the Lord's anointed is before him" (1 Sam. 16:6). God spoke to Samuel and said, "This is not the one. I have refused him," for he said, "The Lord seeth not as man seeth: for man looketh on the outward appearance, but the Lord looketh upon the heart" (v. 7).

God's judgment of us is initially important because it is valid. God's Word concerning us is important because God sees us as we are. Man sees what we do: God knows why we do it. God knows the motives in our hearts. God knows the condition of our lives before him, so immediately Amos was saying, "Here is what God thinks about you." Now they were listening, and he said, "[You are] the whole family which I brought up from the land of Egypt" (3:1). It is obvious now that he was talking about both the Northern Kingdom of Israel and the Southern Kingdom of Judah, for he said "the whole family." He was referring to the whole chosen family at once, all the twelve tribes. It is interesting that surely as God had brought all the people out of Egypt, his judgment was that all the people had rebelled against him. *All* of the people had turned away from him. How soon we forget!

You would think that after the children of Israel saw Moses raise that rod, and after all the miraculous deliverances out of Egypt, the people would have learned. They saw the wind blow, the waters part, and they marched across the Red Sea on dry ground. When it was burning hot in the noon day, God sent a cloud to cover them; and when it was cold at night, God sent a pillar of fire to keep them warm; and when they were hungry, he sent manna out of the clear, blue sky; and when they were thirsty, he brought water out of the rock. You would think they would never forget, wouldn't you?

But they did. It didn't take long until they were grumbling about being hungry. They grumbled because they didn't like God's food. They didn't like manna. They forgot! Amos wrote: "Here's what God thinks about you." He reminded them that he brought all of them out of Egypt.

God has a right to his conclusion about us. God is entitled to have a word with us because he has delivered us from bondage. You can search history, and you will never find another people like Israel and Judah, his chosen people. No other nation can claim to have the unique touch of God upon them like the Jewish people. God chose them and entered into a covenant with them. He affirmed they were the only ones he had *known*. The word *known* is a word which means more than having a mere intellectual acquaintance with. It means to know intimately, with familiarity. It speaks of a relationship of intimacy between God and his people, and God's message to them, "I have known you in a way I don't know anybody else."

That's true of the Christian today. God is not the Father of all men; he is the Father of those who through faith have been saved through the shed blood of Jesus Christ. There is a sense in which he knows us intimately in a way he does not know any others. There was a deep relationship, and so he attested, "You only have I known" (v. 2). As you read you'd think that God was going to give them some really good news. He wanted them to know what he thought about them; he wanted them to remember that he had brought them up out of Egypt; he had a relationship with them. Therefore, "I will punish you." Is that right? "I will punish you for all your iniquities" (v. 2). Somehow that doesn't go together. God's blessed our nation. We have freedom in our land, churches that are free to preach the gospel. We have been entrusted with the gospel; we are the greatest missionary nation in the world; we have sent the gospel around the world; we are in a unique position with God; God will bless us. But God says, "I will punish you for all your iniquities."

To understand what he means, the word *iniquities* speaks of crookedness. God is straight; man is crooked. God's way is always right. Man has a way of always twisting God's way. The iniquities here indicate a perverting of God's way. Here is what happened. Here was a people who had entered into a unique relationship with God, yet they took God's way and twisted it. They claimed a special privilege, but they did not want the responsibility that went along with it. They did not seem to understand that special privileges always result in special obligations; special grace results in special holiness; special revelation requires special scrutiny; and special love requires special responsiveness. They had perverted God's way, and that's exactly what we've done, isn't it?

I am amazed at how many vices we have claimed are virtues by twisting and perverting the Word of God. God says, "You can't get away from it. You are in a unique relationship with me; you have a responsibility, and I am going to chastise you."

God would not be God if he did not remain true to his word. We have a covenant with God through faith in Jesus Christ today. Back in those days, God had a covenant with Israel. A covenant is an agreement on the part of two parties, a commitment that two individuals, or two groups of individuals, make together. Man may be unfaithful to his responsibilities within the covenant, but God isn't. God will keep his part, and God's part is love, grace, mercy, and blessing; man's part is faithfulness and obedience.

When man falls short of his part, there can be no love that tolerates evil, and there can be no holiness that abides in wickedness. God's faithfulness insures that he will keep his part of the bargain, and the other side of love is discipline and chastisement. God declared he would do it! In 2 Timothy 2:13, Paul taught that even if we don't believe, God is faithful. "He cannot deny himself." You can write it down. God is going to keep his end of the bargain, and we have a responsibility in it.

The second idea I want to share is *repentance*. Notice verse 3: "Can two walk together, except they be agreed?" Now that's a rhetorical question. It is a question that can be answered only one way. The phrase *walk together* means joined together. Can two be joined together? In other words, can two people have harmony if they are disharmonious? The answer is *no*. You cannot walk together in harmony with a person with whom you disagree. God was pleading here for the people to accept his judgment, for the people to declare to him that they had accepted his evaluation. The people had been unresponsive and rebellious. They had perverted and twisted his way; now he called them to change that.

This passage was a clarion call for repentance. The way we can walk in harmony with God is to repent and to confess. *Confess* comes from a compound of two words which mean "to agree with, to say the same thing." God says, "This is a sin," and we agree with him, confessing it to him. The direst necessity in our churches and in our lives is for us to become sensitive to the disobedience in our lives, and to turn in repentance and confession to God's way. We have so soothed ourselves that we no longer feel any sense of guilt. We are able to hold ungodly attitudes and live with indifference and apathy; we are able to condone the rebellion in our hearts. God reminds us that we can't walk with him unless we agree. To find agreement with God involves being perfectly obedient to him, and that begins with repentance and confession.

Now, note the *response* which will come. In verses 4-6 are three challenges to repentance.

> *Will a lion roar in the forest, when he hath no prey? will a young lion cry out in his den, if he have taken nothing? Can a bird fall in a snare upon the earth, where no grain is left for him? shall one take up a snare from the earth, and have taken nothing at all? Shall a trumpet be blown in the city, and the people be not afraid? shall there be evil in a city, and the Lord hath not done it?*

Now there are three questions, and an a and b, to each of these verses. In verse 4, the lion was roaring. The lion roared because he was about to pounce on his victim. In the first part, the lion was roaring. In the second part, the lion was licking his chops. He had pounced upon the victim and was enjoying the spoils. Amos was saying, "There is time; the lion is roaring. You are not yet devoured." In Amos the lion was roaring—God was warning of judgment. Our response must be a response of repentance. Verse 5 asks, "Does a bird walk into a trap when there is no bait there?" The trap's there, but the bird doesn't come down when there is no bait. It is a warning snare. The trap doesn't snap shut unless there is something in it. Here was the warning: Now the snare is shut, and judgment comes.

Verse 6 means that when a trumpet is blown, the people are being warned of coming judgment. At the end Amos asked, "Shall evil come and God not do it?" So there was time; there was hope. The message of the preacher today and prophet then is that there is yet time for us to respond to God. The time comes when God moves in our hearts, dealing with us. Whenever you feel the presence of God in your life, his drawing, convicting power, cherish it. This is God's means of saying, "Now is the time I have chosen for you to commit your life to me." The invitation is extended, and the opportunity is there: respond while you have the impulse.

These verses also reveal another truth about God. Verse 4 tells us that God means what he says. The lion doesn't roar unless he's preparing to pounce. God doesn't tell you he's going to do something merely to scare you. God's threats are not idle.

Verse 5 teaches us that when God's judgment comes it is justified. The bird doesn't fly down into a trap if there is no bait there, and when the bird is ensnared it's his own fault. In fact, *The Living Bible* renders that verse, "A trap doesn't snap shut unless it is stepped on; your punishment is well deserved." When God judges us, it is never unfair. You do not need to fear that God is going to be unjust. But you do need to fear the justice of God. Truthfully, we don't want justice—we want mercy. Mercy is ours through repentance, but if we do not repent, then justice comes, and justice will be fair and right. God will always do what is appropriate, what is right, what is eternally true. Verse 6 relates that God is not mocked. You can't make a fool out of him. God is no absentee landlord in the universe. God has not delegated his authority to anyone else or abdicated his rule and power. God is not mocked, and yet we live as though he were.

That's rather frightening to me because in so many ways we

mock God—by singing songs of praise we don't mean, by lifting prayers that are hypocritical, by pretending to be true to truth we have rejected. We mock him by refusing to obey clear, plain commands from his Word. God will not be mocked. Whatever a person sows, he will reap. God reminded them that when judgment and justice came, he wanted them to know that he did it.

The fourth truth (found in verses 7 and 8) is what I would call *revelation*. "Surely the Lord God will do nothing, but he revealeth his secret unto his servants the prophets. The lion hath roared. Who will not fear? The Lord God hath spoken, who can but prophesy?" "Surely the Lord God will do nothing." That doesn't mean God will do absolutely nothing. The statement actually means that God won't do anything by himself. God is not going to appear on television and say, "The next voice you will hear is God's." What he will do is reveal his secrets to his prophets, and that's how we received the Word of God. That's how we get word from God today—through his Word that was delivered through the intimate relationship of the prophet. He doesn't do it apart from them, but he reveals his secrets unto his servants, the prophets.

Now, there is a key. The phrase *reveals his secrets* could be rendered "opens his fellowship." Think about that for a moment. God opens his fellowship to the prophets. When you see that, you understand why or how God's Word came to us. God's Word did not come to us because a man was walking along one day and Zap! Right out of heaven God hit him, he grabbed a stylus and started writing, his eyes glassy. It came because men were open to the fellowship of God. God moved in those men to reveal his Word. "The Lord God hath spoken, who can but prophesy?"

We are being told today that the Bible is not the Word of God. A statement dated October 1979, coming from a group in Dallas, Texas, stated: "The Bible is not the Word of God. The Bible is a written testimony of that word. A written expression of what the Word of God is. The Word of God is Jesus Christ." That sounds good until you come down to that last statement, "The Word of God is Jesus Christ." But what if you deny the written Word? That's the place you read about and learn about Jesus. Talk about idiocy. Talk about logical consistency. There is no way we can claim that the Bible is not the Word of God and simultaneously say that Jesus is the Word of God, because the place we read about Jesus is in the Bible. Jesus is the living Word (Logos). But the Bible is the written Word of God.

Now the tragedy is: Statements like this did not come out of American atheist headquarters in Austin but from an evangelical church group. The greatest threat to Christianity today is not the atheist, not the agnostic, but the liberal who refuses to stand upon the Word of God and has reduced in his mind the revealed truth of God to simply humanistic expressions.

Here is a lesson on revelation, and Amos is one of the most apropos examples we can find. Look back at the first verse of the first chapter. It starts out by saying: "the words of Amos." Verse 3: "Thus saith the Lord." Verse 6: "Thus saith the Lord." Verse 9: "Thus saith the Lord." Verse 11: "Thus saith the Lord." Verse 13: "Thus saith the Lord." Chapter 2, verse 1: "Thus saith the Lord." Verse 4: "Thus saith the Lord." Verse 6: "Thus saith the Lord."

Wait just a minute. He started out speaking about the words of Amos, but then the words of the Lord. Which was right? Was it the word of God, or was it in the word of Amos?

Here is where revelation is seen. I'll try to explain it to you. This passage reveals to us the exciting truth of biblical revelation—eternal truth from God. God picked men—not simply isolated men whom he made zombies and robots—but he entered into a special fellowship with men who were responsive to his word. "Holy men," Peter declared. "Holy men of God spake as they were moved by the Holy Ghost" (2 Pet. 1:21).

They were holy men in that they desired fellowship with God and entered into that relationship with God.

They did not cease being human; they were never more human than when they were close to God, for God brought Jesus Christ in human form, and he is God's perfect man. When we walk in harmony and fellowship with God we become truly and wonderfully human in our relationship with him. God in fellowship drew these men into an experience of his presence, and then God moved through their humanity to speak exactly what he wanted said.

Amos didn't say, "I *think* God said." He didn't say, "I know what God said, and I'll try to tell you in the best way I can." But he said, "Thus saith the Lord." God spoke through Amos. Amos was a herdsman of sheep from Tekoa and a gatherer of sycamore fruit. He had a country culture and country language. But when he entered into the innermost place of fellowship and harmony with God, God's Spirit moved in him through his compelling personality and through his tremendous dedication. Bathed in the presence of God and the spirit of prayer, Amos recorded exactly what God said. That's the revelation of God. That's why we must listen to what God has to say.

My friend, if you reject what God has said, you are denying the voice of God. Don't expect God to speak audibly to you; he doesn't need to. He's already revealed his Word to you. Our part is to hear the voice of the Lord and to respond to him. What a message! God has said, "I love you so intensely, so completely, that I know you cannot meet my standards of eternal, divine righteousness, so I am sending my own Son, Jesus Christ, to die for you." The cross of Jesus Christ and the revelation of God in him show you to what extremes God will go to win you to himself, to forgive your sins, and to present you eternal life.

"Thus saith the Lord." It is the voice of God we need to hear, and whatever opinions may be raised—whatever teaching may be given from here and there—needs to be placed alongside the

Word of God. That article I quoted earlier also said that the teachings of God need to be compared to the culture and the mores of the time in which we live. That is not true. The Word of God is eternal, the Word of God is timeless, the Word of God is the voice of God spoken to holy men of old who recorded the words of God in their own vernacular. But they preached and wrote exactly what God wanted us to hear. The principles are eternal and timeless, and our part is obedience.

The entire message of Amos is one of warning to a people who enjoyed a unique position with God, but that favor also placed a unique responsibility upon them and us. My dear friend, if you know what to do and don't do it, you are under sore judgment. In Matthew 21:28-30 Jesus related a story of a man who had two sons. He told one of the sons, "Son, go work to-day in my vineyard." The son replied, "I go, sir," and then he didn't do it. The other son he asked to work in the vineyard said, "I will not," but after a bit, he repented and went. Jesus asked which of the sons pleased the father? Which one did the will of his father?

You see, if you know to do the will of God, it doesn't do any good to say "I know," then not do it. It would be better to say, "I won't do it," and then do it than to make an empty sham of a promise that will not be kept. God has spoken clearly. These are critical days. We may indeed be living in days where worship in our churches will not be possible over an extended period of time. How urgent it is that when God speaks, we respond. Your part is to obey God. When God speaks to you, listen to him. During the Transfiguration God spoke concerning Jesus, "This is my beloved Son, in whom I am well pleased; hear ye him" (Matt. 17:5). Listen to him and respond to his voice. God will bless your life and give you cleansing, forgiveness, peace, and all that you desire as you listen. Respond to and obey him.

6
The Results of
God's Judgment
Amos 3:9-15

One of Amos's themes, woven throughout these verses, is: It is possible for God's people to become so rebellious and so insensitive to the purposes of God, that in reality God becomes an *adversary*. That's an incredible thought.

We talk about struggling against Satan, and we have placed great emphasis on the fact that we not be so careless as to fall victim to the power of the devil. But in our intense concern that we not fall into the power of Satan, we have fallen *out of* the power of God. We have found that our purposes, our directions, and our tendencies have not been commensurate with our declaration of faith. We have not been consistent with the relationship we claim with Christ. In Isaiah 63:10 the prophet proclaimed, "But they rebelled, and vexed his holy spirit: therefore he was turned to be their enemy, and he fought against them."

It is amazing that the people of God should suddenly find themselves pitted against God. But throughout Amos and in this passage we have the reminder of God's judgment upon his people. It is addressed to the chosen people, the covenant people, those who had committed themselves to God in some fashion, to the extent that they were called the people of God.

First, I want you to behold *the drama*. It's almost as though Amos was putting together a vast audience for a dramatic presentation. Notice verse 9, "Publish in the palaces at Ashdod, and in the palaces in the land of Egypt, and say, Assemble yourselves upon the mountains of Samaria." He called a huge gathering to view what was taking place and also summoned the heathen nations surrounding Israel. What a terrifying thought for Israel that heathen nations would sit in judgment of Israel!

God's people had received a special revelation from God; they had prophets sent to them; they had the Word of God proclaimed to them; they had entered into a covenant relationship with God. They were the recipients of a divine revelation; surrounding them were their hateful enemies—pagan, heathen people. A prophet of Israel had never gone to Ashdod, Assyria or Egypt. Those heathens had never had a revelation from God proclaimed to them. Those ungodly nations in opposition to the purposes of God, it would seem, would now become judges of the people of God.

What a fearful sight it was! Those enemies were gathering to judge Israel, God's covenant people. Nothing could have been darker than that. Yet, I could not read that without reminding myself that if God could use the godless lands of Assyria and Egypt in anicent times, certainly God could use Russia, Red China, or whomever to judge his people today. We must be reminded that God will not tolerate disobedience from his people, and this passage causes us to see the judgment of God upon his disobedient covenant people. So, Amos cried, "Publish in the palaces at Ashdod, and in the palaces in the land of Egypt, and say, Assemble yourselves upon the mountains of Samaria, and behold the great tumults in the midst thereof, and the oppressed in the midst thereof" (3:9).

Here was the picture. Israel was in a time of unprecedented prosperity. It seemed everybody was doing well. They had peace. In the past, Assyria had rushed down from the north and destroyed the land, and Egypt attacked from the south. It had seemed Israel was sort of a no-man's land, and whoever became strongest—Egypt or Assyria—would run right over Israel. Israel was always being persecuted and oppressed. Now, however, there was peace, harmony, and prosperity. They were not being oppressed from the north or south. They were in an unprecedented period of peace, luxury, and affluence.

Surely in such a time the people would have paused and thanked God for it. "God, thank you that we have peace. Thank you that we have things necessary for life—and luxuries, too." Instead the people used their prosperity and peace to go farther and farther away from God, to reject him, his purposes, and his plan. In the midst of prosperity, there was great unrest and insecurity despite great material advance; there was tremendous upheaval in the land.

Can we identify with that? We've never known a period of peace like we've enjoyed these last few years. God has given us relative ease and there has been a prosperity unprecedented, unparalleled in the world. Yet, in our land there is a gnawing sense of unrest, of insecurity, and of upheaval that is tearing at the fiber of our society. That was also the tragedy that unfolded in ancient Israel. Just as the heathen enemies of Israel gathered 'round to observe the drama acted out, so like vultures around their prey Communist lands are surrounding America.

It has been declared that we will be the last vestige of freedom to fall. Around us our enemies are watching the drama taking place. Instead of falling on our knees before God who alone can redeem and heal our land, we are doing exactly as they did in Israel. We're simply going our way, looking out for ourselves, and disregarding the purposes of God for our lives. That is the drama unfolding today, and it is a tragedy of no little degree.

Further in the passage we see not only the drama, but *the disobedience* of the people. Verse 10 goes, "They know not to do right, saith the Lord, who store up violence and robbery in their palaces." Verses 13 and 14: "Hear ye, and testify in the house of Jacob, saith the Lord God, the God of hosts, That in the day that I shall visit the transgressions of Israel upon him I shall also visit the altars of Bethel; and the thorns of the altar shall be cut off, and fall to the ground."

Now, observe the disobedience. "They know not to do right."

The people had become so insensitive to the words of God that they did not even know how to do right. They had lost their capacity to do right. They could no longer discern the will of God. Their vaulted prosperity and their perilous peace, had wrought a barrier between them and God. It had driven a wedge between the people and their God, but also among themselves, for the land was torn by class and levels of society.

They had lost viable contact with God. Their materialism had caused them to decay, sapping their strength. It had made them incapable of doing right, and I believe that's still happening. I worry about America today because we have had it so easy. I'm not sure we're any longer capable of rising to a gigantic challenge with courage to match. You know why the Japanese attacked Pearl Harbor? Their leaders told us they attacked because they did not believe the Americans had the courage to retaliate. But we did! I'm not sure we will again. We've lost our character, our courage, our reason to stand upon principles. We lean on comfort and ease. Most everyone wants to do his own thing, and we have built a materialistic society to the total disregard of God. It has robbed us of moral and spiritual perception. We don't know how to do right, and that's exactly what happened in the disobedience of Israel.

Next, view the second aspect of their disobedience. They "store up violence and robbery in their palaces." In that phrase is a meaning hidden from the casual reader. At first glance it seems they do nothing but violence and robbery. They robbed one another; they were violent, they had a crime-ridden society, and they were building up an "escrow" of robbery and violence. But I think Amos was saying more than that. Actually they were building up robbery and violence, and those crimes were going to become the very means of their own destruction. Just as they were stealing from one another and violently attacking one another, so an enemy would come in with robbery and violence and do exactly the same to them. The enemy would steal and use violence to the destruction of Israel.

There is a boomerang effect to sin. When you sin, there is built into that very sin a boomerang that shall return in judgment. "The soul that sinneth, it shall die" (Ezek. 18:4). "Sin, when it is finished, bringeth forth death" (James 1:15). Sin has within the act or attitude itself the seeds of self-destruction. Sin is suicide. Anyway you look at it, everytime you sin you die a little bit. Everytime you sin, there is riveted into your character and life the bolts of your own judgment—and that is Amos's warning. Their disobedience was going to be used to punish them.

In verse 13 he wrote, "Hear ye, and testify in the house of Jacob, saith the Lord God, the God of hosts." I wondered about that: Why did he call it the house of Jacob? This was the land of Israel. Why the house of Jacob? It was an ancestral title. It was like when my mother wanted me to straighten up and do right. She would say, "Now, Jimmy, you remember what your daddy said." Daddy was a preacher, but she really got to me with, "Now, Jimmy, your dad and your granddaddy were both preachers, and you remember what your granddad said." She would carry me back to the past.

That's precisely what Amos was doing. He carried them back to make them remember from whence they had come. "Remember who you are," he was saying, "You're not just like Ashdod, Assyria, and Egypt. You're the house of Jacob, the children of God. You have a special privilege." He reminded them who they were, who they belonged to, and where they came from. I believe we must be reminded who we are. We're children of the King; we're heirs of God and joint-heirs with Christ Jesus. We ought to live like it, stand like it; act like it. We ought to conduct our lives based upon the principles of God's Word. He was reminding them who they really were.

God warned in verse 14, "I shall visit the transgressions of Israel upon him." He was not picking out any particular day. He said, "In the day." He was predicting that judgment was certain. He was not pointing out a time, but he was saying judgment is inevitable. The word *transgression* gives us a key to the meaning of this message. *Transgression* means willful disobedience to the will of God. God was not going to allow the people to disobey him willfully, knowing that they shouldn't do it. He would not allow the people to go on indefinitely in their willful disobedience to the known will of God. They had become callous towards each other and uncaring about social justice. They had ceased to love God and to care for the things of God, and their forgetfulness, callousness, and rebellion were transgressions before God.

At this point is where we have the direst need in America today—we're blatantly disobedient to the will of God. We can talk all we want about how we need to know more biblical truth. We've created a mass of people who want to study their Bibles and learn more. I'm happy about their desire, but the crying need is for us to do what we know to do. One's problem with the Scriptures is not what he doesn't understand; it's what one understands and refuses to do. And transgression is a known disobedience. God is pleading with us, challenging us, calling us. Do what you know to do. That's our difficulty. It reminds me of the college student who came home to his farmer dad and tried to tell him how to be a better farmer. His student son was telling him everything he learned at college, and after a while the father waved him off and said, "Ah, Son, I already know how to do more than I do."

We're all kind of like that, aren't we? We know to do more than we do, and God is going to lose patience with us someday; he's going to call a halt. That's what Amos wrote about Israel, "I will visit your transgression upon you. I will come in judgment because you persist in disobeying me."

Amos then talked about "the altars of Bethel: and the horns of the altar shall be cut off, and fall to the ground" (v. 14). First

Kings 12:28 records that Jeroboam set up two golden calves in Samaria. The reason was that he wanted to make religion more convenient for the people (v. 27). It was an awful long trip to Jerusalem, and he wanted his subjects to be able to worship in Samaria. So he built two golden calves with horns, the lengthy horns themselves becoming the symbols of superstition and mock religious concern. The idea was: if you could only hold onto the horns of the altar, you would be protected. You would find divine provision for your needs and protection in whatever form you wanted. So a great deal of mystery surrounded the horns of the altar.

Jeroboam had built a calf with golden horns, and it was to be the pedestal upon which the invisible God sat, but by and by the visible took the place of the invisible. In time the people became fixed to the golden bull calf, and they identified God with that. After all of their meticulous ritualism and formalism which centered around the worship in Samaria, where the bull calf with the golden horns became central, God chided, "I'm even going to visit the altars of Bethel, and the horns shall fall to the ground." Even their heretical religion would be pulled away from them as the crutch upon which they tried to lean. What had happened was: True religion had become lost in formalism and ritualism. True theology and religion had been compromised, and Jehovah had become identified with the bull calf. The mind of mere man had supplanted the mind of God. Revelation had been adapted, distorted, and trimmed until it matched human understanding. That was their disobedience, and how careful we must be lest we let our religion be denigrated into human understanding.

Secular humanism claims that whatever a man thinks is right. Now, you can couch it with any terms you wish, but that's basically what we face in our nation. It expresses itself in politics, in philanthropy, in philosophy, and in theology. In theology humanism states that the Word of God is the product of man's concern for God and is man's attempt to explain his concept of God. Little by little, then, we pull away from the authoritative Scriptures, and we make the mind, the determination, and the judgment of man the basis on which we live. That's exactly what happened in Israel. The mind of man had replaced the mind of God and had become the criterion by which society and worship were judged.

It was a disobedience then and still is today. God has given us his Word. It is a Word to be believed, to be trusted, and to be obeyed. We have a tremendous opportunity in America to be responsive to the claims and to the call of God for our lives.

Third, I want you to notice *the destruction* which accompanied this judgment. Verses 11, 12, and 15 describe it.

> *Therefore thus saith the Lord; An adversary there shall be even round about the land; and he shall bring down thy strength from thee, and thy palaces shall be spoiled. Thus saith the Lord; As the shepherd taketh out of the mouth of the lion two legs, or a piece of an ear; so shall the children of Israel be taken out that dwell in Samaria in the corner of bed, and in Damascus in a couch . . . And I will smite the winter house with the summer house; and the houses of ivory shall perish, and the great houses shall have an end, saith the Lord.*

Now look at several ideas about the destruction. First of all Amos said an *"adversary"* will come. It has to come, folks. Anytime you live like Israel did, an adversary will appear. God will not tolerate our rebellion. God will not let the people who claim his name live in disobedience. The adversary is bound to come against such a land. If God would move in judgment then because of their disobedience to him, how can he fail to bring judgment upon America? How can he fail to send an adversary to the U.S. That adversary is going to bring down the strength from you, and your homes shall be spoiled. When the blow falls, it's not going to be a light one. When God comes in judgment and the axe falls, it will be a severe judgment. Our defenses will be demolished and the fortresses will be plundered. The judgment of God is a complete judgment.

Amos continued in verse 12 by talking about *the shepherd*. As I read that I wondered; *It seems kind of strange.* "As the shepherd taketh out of the mouth of the lion two legs, or a piece of an ear." I couldn't figure that out, and then it dawned on me. The shepherd had to prove that he didn't take the lamb for himself, and so anytime a wild animal attacked the flock—in order to keep from having to pay for the loss—the shepherd had to produce evidence that an animal had invaded the flock, so he'd get a piece of an ear, a leg or whatever was left, and he'd show it to the owners, thus exonerating himself. Now, that was all right for the shepherd, but it didn't do much for the sheep, did it? Such a rescue is really no rescue at all, is it? What sheep could exist with an ear and a piece of a leg left?

Obviously the destruction was devastating. There are some who feel Amos meant a remnant would be saved out of Israel. Of course, there always has been a remnant down through history, and if you study through the Old Testament there is the concept of the remnant. To me that's not what he's talking about here. I believe he's talking about the fact that destruction is coming; it would be a sad, solemn, and deadly destruction. There will be only small evidences of what once was. Now, read what he said about the people: "So shall the children of Israel." Now bear in mind, these were God's people, people of the covenant, and God had revealed himself to their forefathers. He delivered them from slavery, through the wilderness, and into the Prom- ised Land. These were covenant people, the people of God. The children of Israel would be taken in a corner of a bed, in a couch. Now listen to this.

He was describing the evidence of a civilization, the legacy of the people of God to the future, and all that would remain would be a few beds, couches, and pillars. This would be characteristic of the lives and habits of the people who called themselves the people of God, and yet their lives were characterized by sensuality, luxury, idleness, and bodily care. There was no evidence that the people of God had any hunger for him. There was no evidence that they ever fell on their knees in earnest prayer or that they ever revered and obeyed the Word of God when their legacy was written for the future. When the remains of God's judgment were sifted through, all you would be able to find was evidence that they were a sensual, materialistic culture with virtually no thought of God. And these were the people of God! Imagine it! This evidence was coming from people who claimed they belonged to God, but they had become so wrapped up in living for their own comfort, for their own selves, that the only evidence left after God's judgment would be their sensuality. When the history of the 1980s is recorded, I wonder if it will record of this so-called Christian nation evidence of its hunger of God, seeking after his presence, standing for his purposes and holiness. Or will the record be simply notations and artifacts of materialism, sensuality, and comfort—with no concern for the things of eternity? I could not help but weep as I read of a nation whose God was the Lord and which became so disobedient and so rebellious to the known will of God that, when her testimony was given to her children who would be in captivity, it would be an account of a nation which lived only for itself, for the satisfaction of sensual pleasure, and for the things of temporary existence.

God said, "I will smite the winter house with the summer house; and the houses of ivory shall perish, and the great houses shall have an end, saith the Lord" (3:15). All the luxury would be gone—"houses of ivory." It occurred to me that even Solomon had only a throne of ivory, but these folks had houses of ivory. Wealth, luxury, and prosperity had robbed them of their spiritual strength and their reason to exist. You see, heresy never stands idle. It always moves on to produce godlessness, materialism, and an ostentatious people. When religion is powerless, all of society is powerless. When the house of God falls, every house falls.

The tragic fact was: The people in Amos's day were trying to justify their style of living on the basis that it was evidence God was blessing them. They believed that prosperity was a sign that God was blessing them. And don't we do the same? When we ask God to bless us, most of the time we're thinking about having enough money to get what we want and do what we want to do—have the kind of house and car we want. God has really blessed us. We don't hear much about spiritual blessings; we think a lot about material blessings.

The people in Amos's day just knew that since they were so prosperous, God was blessing them. Hear me. Prosperity is not a sign of the blessing of God. Now God may bless you with prosperity, but it is not an unequivocal sign of God's blessings. In every culture some of the most godless people have been the most prosperous. We need to be careful that we don't attribute the prosperity and progress of America as being a sign of the blessings of God. It may be, in fact, exactly the opposite. Not many of us can stand prosperity. It cuts the heart out; it removes the character. We become too fearful of what we might lose. You see, the person who has already lost all doesn't care what happens next, and that's why the devil fears a person who's abandoned everything to God. A person who's already given it all to God has nothing left to lose, and he's dangerous to the devil and the forces of evil.

That's why there's such tremendous pressure, in my judgment, in the religious world to keep us confined to a certain pattern. There is a wicked force to cause us to conform and to continue with traditional, ritualistic, formalistic religious worship, rather than recklessly serving God. I pray God will let our churches be those that serve God with reckless abandon, daring for God, reaching for the sky, because God has promised to give it to us and to be in it with us as we serve him. Let's not be content merely trying to protect what we have—because if we really believe God gave it to us, we'll have to trust him to protect it and to provide for us.

The truth is that we've become selfish and self-centered as a people. We've become soft and indulgent; we've become sensual and extravagant, luxury-seeking, leisure-seeking. I personally think that one of the best things that may happen would be: for our national situation to become desperate enough to drive us back to God. It's the only hope we have.

God says, "When you willfully disobey me, then I will visit your transgressions upon you." There's an adversary waiting in the wings. God has told us what to do. There's no time to waste, no time to wait until tomorrow. We're not merely treading water and playing games; we're engaged in a combat of eternal consequences; we wrestle not against flesh and blood but against principalities and powers. In God's power we wrestle and struggle in the eternal conflict our Lord has thrust us into, and our role is to be obedient. We must trust and obey—or judgment is certain to fall!

7
Corruption and Ecclesiasticism
(Amos 4:1-5)

Amos presented nothing new in Amos 4:1-5. He had been gathering facts, and it seems as though he was going to draw some sharply focused pictures based on those facts. He reminded the people of the responsibility they had toward God, of the certainty of God's judgment upon a land and a people who forgot God.

Putting all of this together, he did so in two pictures in these verses. First he pictured wealthy, affluent homes of Samaria, and then he depicted their worship centers: their shrines in Bethel and Gilgal. There are three elements, as I see them, in these five verses. We need to look at them in order to understand properly the message of Amos for us.

First, in verse 1, there is a description of sensuous living. "Hear this word, ye kine of Bashan." *Kine* means cows—or if you grew up on a farm, heifers. I have learned that there is a difference between a heifer and a bull (you can tell I didn't grow up on a farm). That's the word here—cows, and it speaks of the self-indulgent, slothful women of Samaria.

The cows of Bashan would represent the finest herds in the land. Bashan is in the area east of the Jordan River and to the north of the Yarmuck River. It is a vast, grassy plain which produced some of the healthiest cattle in the world. The cows of Bashan were sleek, well-proportioned, well-fed, thoroughbred, pedigreed animals. They had all of the physical provisions for their physical needs; they lived for their appetites and provisions, for themselves and their narcissism. They were self-centered, bent on sensual satisfaction without a spiritual dimension to their lives.

Amos described a culture which had forgotten God, a society which made the things of the world its primary pursuit—not the things of God. He depicted a people who no longer had a spirit of worship. Whenever a nation eliminates God from its perspective, soon nothing has lasting value. Israel was a sensate society.

The "kine of Bashan" in the mountain of Samaria oppressed the poor and crushed the needy. The insatiable lusts of those wives caused their weak husbands to use every drastic measure to enlarge their incomes, thus providing sensuality and luxury for their wives. Those men gave their selfish wives what they wanted—at the dire expense of others. Here was an account of those who thrive on the miseries of others. They were devoid of compassion.

Do you notice the downward steps? When you place yourselves in a dimension that bypasses God, the logical result is a calloused, insensitive society without compassion for the downtrodden, poor, and needy. Here were unscrupulous people who crushed and oppressed the poor in order to appease their own hunger. They commanded their "masters," "Bring and let us drink" (v. 1). The word *masters* here could be translated "lords." Who was he talking about? The kine of Bashan's husbands. Here Amos's message drips with sarcasm. The phrase, "Bring, and let us drink," speaks of parties, banquets, feasts, and perhaps orgies. Their life-style involved extravagance, gluttony, and giving of oneself to pleasure-seeking. "They say to their lords [husbands]" do this and do that.

There was no question of who wore the pants in those families—and who ran their society. They lived for luxury, not for necessity; for kicks, not for spiritual life. Such is invariably the response of a society which has no spiritual dimension.

Right now I believe this nation faces the most sinister danger in its history. For many years we have enjoyed such physical and material prosperity and affluence that we may have felt it is unnecessary to have a spiritual dimension. When we descend to that nadir, we have become the kind of society described in verse 1—sensual living.

In verse 2 and 3 we see what I would call security lost. The reason a person can live sensually is because of a false sense of security—that he will always have the opportunity to get what he wants, that he will always be strong, that he will always have prosperity. In these verses is a description of God's judgment. God condemned them because they were devoid of a spiritual commitment and dimension.

God pulled the rug out from under them. He removed their security; they fell into captivity and lost the very things they had exploited. The baubles around which they had built their lives were snatched away from them. Nothing was left but the shambles.

Notice how Amos handled the matter. He started off with a statement: "The Lord hath sworn." That is a play on words. In verse 1 he wrote that the women told their "masters" what to do; then the "masters" oppressed the poor and crushed the needy. He then indicated, in essence, "There is another Lord who must be heard. There is another Lord who will not be silenced. The Lord God has a word to say. He must speak his piece." Anytime a society builds itself up as being lord and master, and self-sufficient, there will always be a forthcoming word from the Lord God.

"The Lord God hath sworn by his holiness" (v. 2). There are several concepts in this verse. God had taken an oath. Why take an oath? An oath is taken as testimony that something is true, and it gives assurance. In a court of law you "swear" (or change the wording to "promise") to tell the truth. That is done to help insure the honesty and accuracy of the testimony. If one's testimony is found to be untruthful, perjury may be the result.

An oath is an assurance. We often say, "Oh, I promise you that's true." If they're a little skeptical, you might say, "I promise you on my mother's grave" or "on a stack of Bibles." In court you put your left hand on the Bible and your right upheld toward heaven, and you "promise to tell the whole truth and nothing but the truth, so help you God." God and his veracity are involved in the court oath. An oath is a frightful declaration.

"The Lord God hath sworn by his holiness." There are two aspects to holiness. First of all, holiness is the quality which makes God, God—sets him apart, makes him different from mankind. That's the first connotation of holiness—God is different.

God is not limited by human personality, human ingenuity, or human energy. God is of a different character and nature. In a sense, holiness *is* God. He is the personalizing spiritually of holiness. When God swears by his holiness, he swears upon his own character and nature.

The second aspect of holiness is this: Holiness makes him a particular kind of God. Yes, he is different, but that difference is dramatically evidenced by the nature of that difference. He is holy. He is moral purity.

What makes God a being to whom reverence, awe, and worship are due is his holiness. We do not tremble before God merely because of our humanity in contrast to his omnipotence. Rather, we tremble before him because of our sin in the presence of One with perfect moral purity. I do not primarily revere God for his strength—but for his holiness. That was true of Adam and Eve, if you will recall. Adam did not seem to reverence God because God was more powerful or divine in contrast to Adam's humanity. He did not seem to fear God because of his wisdom or strength. But Genesis 3:8 declares that Adam was afraid of God when he stood before God as a sinner.

Nothing could be more compelling than God's oath. This was a violent oath. The force God placed in this oath is inconceivable to our finite minds. God swore by his nature, by who he is and what he is. God wanted to make sure that the people listened. Surely the words God was about to speak were earth-shattering. What was his message?

"Lo, the days shall come upon you" (v. 2). God had placed his existence, character, and nature on the line. God delivered the verbal blow which would become a concrete reality. "My judgment is coming upon you." Amos deals with society in verse 1 and their hypocritical religious observances in verses 4 and 5. He described a people that was exclusive—they cared only for themselves and their gratification. Their religion was consistent with their life-style—cold, unfeeling, uncompassionate, self-centered, and devoid of God. God rightfully swore that judgment was coming. The day of accountability was imminent. There is no escape from that truth.

"Be not deceived; God is not mocked: for whatsoever a man soweth, that shall he also reap" (Gal. 6:7). In Numbers 32:23 Moses warned, "Be sure your sin will find you out."

It is inexorably woven into the fabric of society: God will not allow a civilization to be built around itself to his exclusion without moving in judgment upon it. Their security would be lost. "He will take you away with hooks, and your posterity with fishhooks" (v. 2b). The real bovines of Bashan were led around by hooks and ropes. Just as those cows were herded and pulled by the hooks in their noses, so would the Israelites be carried away captive.

"Ye shall go out at the breaches, and . . . ye shall cast them into the palace" (v. 3). He was referring to gaps in the wall of the city. In other words, there wouldn't be any need to go through the gate, because there would be huge holes in the wall. Destruction would descend and there would be no security. This picture carried with it the idea of the people's being led away as cattle from a stock pen. They would be goaded through breakdowns in the protective wall which had surrounded them.

In verses 4 and 5 Amos spoke about spiritual license or licentiousness in their worship services. "Come to Beth-el, and transgress." That doesn't seem to mesh—he was actually saying, "Come to church and sin." There it is: "At Gilgal multiply transgression." They were sinning all the more by coming to the shrines without genuine repentance. They were rebelling against God.

Here we have the portrait of people going through the motions without committing their lives to the Lord. They had become faithful to religious ritual and formalism but had lost the heart and genuine meaning of it all. Amos was a master of irony, sarcasm, and satire. He mocked their calls to worship. "Come to Beth-el." "Come to Gilgal." Who knows? Maybe they sang songs of pilgrimage and commitment.

Amos trenchantly exposed their sham in worship. Rather than deep-down worship, they were multiplying their sins. Amos laughed at their religious and ritualistic faithfulness. They were so punctual. They stood at the right time. They knelt precisely when they should. But they were "playing church." They did all the proper things, but sinned through their pious pretensions.

They sacrificed every morning; they gave tithes; they were rigidly careful about tending to every minute detail. They were certainly akin to the Pharisees of Jesus' day.

Hear me. All of us have our rituals. Some churches have the ritual of informality, but it's a ritual just the same. I've heard certain church members brag, "We don't have a bulletin; we just let the Spirit lead." That's fine, but that's also a ritual. Whatever form our worship assumes is a ritual. It can become formalism. We should understand the intent of form and ritual. What we do in worship—pray, sing, praise, preach, present our tithes and offerings, whatever—should be a telescope. We should look through those things, not at them. Any activity can become hollow, sinful, and vain if it does not point us to the Holy God.

If we aren't careful we'll fall into the trap of the Samaritans.

They looked at their rituals rather than through them. When the choir sings we should not merely rejoice in the harmony and the "joyful sound," but the choir should direct our ears and hearts to the God of glory. Their singing should result in a deeper relationship with God. All of our activities in worship should enable us to touch "the hem of his garment."

There is no worship until there is an encounter with the living God. When we attend church, if we do not enter into a new experience with God and a fresh touch of His Spirit upon our lives, we have not worshiped. When our worship ceases to operate like a telescope, we begin to fall into all kinds of heresy and compromise. Notice in verse 5: "Offer a sacrifice of thanksgiving with leaven." The law of Moses strictly forbade the use of leaven, but somehow in Israel they had decided to make the sacrifice a thanksgiving offering with leaven. That was blatantly in contradiction to the Mosaic law.

When our rituals become ends unto themselves, and we forget what they are for, we fall prey to sin and bring in elements which are forbidden by God. Wrap your mind around that! We begin to incorporate forbidden elements and procedures into our worship services. We compromise the form itself, and we also compromise the essence and meaning of worship. The Samaritans injected the forbidden into their worship practices.

Amos instructed, "Proclaim and publish the free offerings" (v. 5). These were the free-will offerings. They were to be personal between the individual and God. But the people began to make a show of their giving. One perversion of worship is when we want people to give us credit for our offerings, our singing, our playing an instrument. According to Jesus: When we want people to know, we do our alms before men, and they praise us. That constitutes our reward but nullifies a reward from our Heavenly Father.

"Proclaim and publish the free offerings: for this liketh you." In other words, "You love to make a show of your giving. You

love to brag and boast about it. You are proud of yourselves."
They had digressed into an ostentatious motive for worship.
Such showiness reveals corrupted reasons for going to church,
participating in the activities, and giving. We must realize that
our worship must issue forth from hearts that genuinely long for
God.

The people of the Northern Kingdom had patterned their
worship after their life-styles. Their worship had become compromised and perverted, so they built their worship upon
pleasing self. They lost sight of worship as being commanded
and ordained of God.

Look at the religious privileges they had. They had a house of
worship to attend, sacrifices to offer, and other advantages. So do
most of us—well-appointed church buildings, advanced equip-
ment, up-to-date methods, and many other aids. They had
religious duties, obligations, and tithes. They had religious
joys—thanksgiving to offer, gratitude to present, and praise to
give Almighty God. They had "a form of godliness," to use
Paul's wording, but denied the power thereof. They had a
modicum of religious devotion. Yet, Amos concluded that there
was a heavy pointlessness to their religious practices. It was
unreal and futile to the mind of God. It was harmful to the
worshipers because they were in the throes of sin—and by and
large unaware of their abysmal condition.

People should come to church to be relieved of sin, not to
commit more sin; to have their burdens lifted, not to have
heavier burdens piled on. Their form of worship was so formalistic and humanistic, it had become totally twisted. They came to
worship but actually perpetuated their rebellion against God.
They left the place of worship more burdened than when they
came.

Oh, they were religious. They moved beyond the demands of
the law and offered sacrifices every morning. Yet, all of their
formalities were transgressions, for there was the absence of the

Spirit of God. We must remember that in true worship, there is always the touch of God's hand. Worship can become the vehicle through which we are transported into "the heavenlies." In genuine worship we lay hold on God afresh. We enter into a new relationship with him, by which we are confronted with our sins, and in the conviction of the Holy Spirit, confess them to the Father. Thus, we go away with a new sense of forgiveness and reality. That should be the desire and dream of our worship together—and that is the deep desire of God's heart.

Read the remainder of chapter 4, and you will discover that five times, starting in verse 6, this phrase appears: "Yet have ye not returned unto me, saith the Lord." See also verses 8, 9, 10, and 11. Through Amos, God was telling the people, "I did this to show my love, even though you were rebellious—to draw you to me. Still you have not returned unto me!"

The call of God for judgment—the warning of God in a stern, dramatic oath, when God swears by his holiness that judgment is coming—is always preceded by his compassionate appeal for us to receive his mercy and grace. God longs to cleanse and forgive us. He does not delight in the punishment people receive for their sins. He pines for a response to his gracious invitation.

But there must be a response on the part of the people. The people of Amos's era had transgressed beyond mercy. Within a few years from his prophecy, their society would come crashing down. Amos's dreadful predictions became nightmarish realities as the Northern Kingdom was carried away into captivity by the cruel Assyrians.

In this day God is giving us an unparalleled opportunity to have a renewed relationship with him, standing on his Word and building a society with a spiritual dimension—a society not predicated on sensuality and rebellion. This may be our last chance to claim the best of God for our lives and our nation!

8
Divine Warnings in Nature
(Amos 4:6-13)

Here is a tremendously important passage of Scripture, perhaps one of the most encouraging, blessed portions of God's
Word.

Here Amos was talking about trouble, crisis, disappointments,
calamity, depression, disaster, heartache, grief, and sorrow! The
aforementioned blights touch all of us, but God is mindful, and
Amos in this passage deals with the relationship of God to the
problems of this world.

The fact immediately clear is: This is a story of God. God is
the central character. It starts off with these words, "And I have
also given. . . ." God was speaking, and the first-person singular
verb was used in verse 6, and that verb is repeated nine times.
These verbs speak concerning the action of God. As we read
through this passage of Scripture we are made aware that God is
central. God's activity is also seen in contrast to the activity of the
people. In the verses previously preceding these, there is a
catalog of the religious activities of the people. These were
exceedingly busy people, busy making money and storing up for
the future. They had been busy being religious. They had
sophisticated rituals, stilted formalism, and emphasis on worship
so-called.

It was as though God had said, "You have been very busy, and
I'm aware of that, but I've been busy, too." The words in verse 6
point back. Just as the people had been busy doing this and that,
giving themselves to materialism and the god of mammon which

cannot endure, God said, "I've been busy." Then the prophet records God's activities.

It is significant that in all this busy-ness (verses 4-5) there is no testimony that they had ever offered a sin offering. The sin offering was the evidence of confession and repentance, a designated offering which was set apart as a means of expressing repentance and contrition of the hearts of individuals, asking God for a cleansing and forgiveness. In fact, in the proper order of the Old Testament sacrificial system, you could not give an offering of sacrifice for thanksgiving or praise until you had made a sin offering. Yet, in the catalog of the people's busy-ness there is no evidence of repentance. This picture is more clearly seen when we notice that the thanksgiving sacrifice which they did make, as recorded in verse 5, was made with leaven. The law strictly forbade leaven to be used. What they had done— because of a lack of repentance on their part, because their religion was largely to please themselves, to gratify their own flesh, to get what they wanted, to satisfy their own needs—was add a forbidden thing to the worship of God. Now all of their activity is here. Starting in verse 6 we have the activity of God as he was calling his people to repentance and to return to him.

Verses 6 through 11 give us a description of what God was doing. *Activity* is the word. God was moving in nature. God will never let his people perish without a witness being given. In Acts 14, Luke the inspired writer made this manifestly clear. In essence, he wrote that God permitted all the nations to go on their own, and yet he didn't leave himself without a witness. Acts 14:17 refers to the witness that God had given in nature.

Amos views all of God's activities in nature as a direct testimony. Whether God's activity or visitation is interpreted as chastisement or punishment, or whether it is seen as grace and mercy, God intends everything for the purpose of bringing salvation, to bring his people to himself. It is the reason for his operation in nature. This passage lists what God has done to bring people to him.

First of all, God declared, "I have given you cleanness of teeth and want of bread," and it apparently had become a nationwide matter. This speaks of a famine; want of bread refers to the fact that they lacked sufficient food. It had swept the nation. Recession, as I write these words, is upon our land. Unemployment is the highest since The Great Depression. The situation is becoming urgent as the unemployment lines lengthen and as many lack necessary food.

God declared, I gave you famine, yet you have not returned unto me." He withheld the rain. The picture is that the rain stopped three months prior to the harvest. That meant that the latter rains which came during the time immediately preceding the harvest were stopped. God said I sent a drought upon the cities. One city would have some water and another wouldn't. The people in two or three cities would wander into one city. The word wander here means to stagger. They came looking for help unto the cities but did not find it.

God said, "I have sent all of this upon you, and yet you have not returned to me." Verse 9 says, "I have smitten you with blasting and mildew." Blasting here describes the scorching heat of the desert winds that sweep out of the arid, barren waste surrounding the area. That sirocco would blow into the crop fields and would wither and destroy the crops. Often would come behind the blasting, scorching wind of the desert, a mildew, that would add further damage to the crop. Then he spoke of the palmerworm and the locusts which came behind the mildew. God said, "I sent it all and yet you have not returned me."

Verse 10 states, "I sent among you pestilence." The word *pestilence* was a common Hebrew word. It is used fifty times in the Old Testament and speaks of the acts of God in judgment upon the people. This pestilence was "after the manner of Egypt," the judgment of God upon Egypt through the plagues that were sent. Then Amos wrote about war and the slaying of their young men on the battlefield. The pestilence came, and "yet have ye not returned unto me." Verse 11 spoke of natural catastrophe. "I have overthrown some of you as Sodom and Gomorrah, and ye were as a firebrand plucked out of the burning." That could refer to earthquakes which accompanied the destruction of Sodom and Gomorrah, volcanic eruptions. Or it could refer to any natural disaster. God said, "I sent that to you, and yet you have not returned unto me."

All the troubles of life are listed here in one form or another—lack of health, pestilence and disaster, every natural occurrence, every accident and tragedy, every heartache.

Here is what Amos said: God is behind all of them. How do you react to that? Think about it a minute. Does it make you mad? Any bitterness? Problems come into your life, and God sent them! Now that may cause you to recoil a little bit. Our natural tendency would be to say, "Well, I don't want a God like that; I don't want a God who would do such a thing! How could a loving God do that?" Wait a minute, if that's your response, if that's my response, we are saying that we don't want a God any smarter than we are. We don't want a God who ever does anything we don't fully understand. We don't want a God who ever reaches beyond our intelligence. We cannot comprehend how God could do that, but Amos said those matters were the activity of God in their midst.

There is something tremendously encouraging about that, because what Amos was saying, "Nothing takes us away from God's purposes. Nothing happens to us that God doesn't use to strengthen and bless us. That is also the New Testament discovery and interpretation. The Apostle Paul in Romans 8:28 said, "All things work together for good to them that love God, to them who are the called according to his purpose." That means God will never let anything detour his purposes for you. *All* is a little word but it is an inclusive word. It involves everything that happens. Then the remaining portion of Romans 8 describes the things we think would normally separate us—distress, nakedness, peril, sword, danger, all of those things. Yet, Paul concluded, nothing can "separate us from the love of Christ."

That means we can look into the eye of the storm and see the Father. We can stare into the mouth of adversity, into the heart of sorrow and sadness, and we can view the distresses of this life— and know that somehow, though we may not fathom it, God is in the midst of it. God is involved in it. Directly or indirectly, God has sent it into our lives, either through his perfect will or his permissive will. It is intended to draw us to him. That's good news! Because everyone of us hurts and knows sadness. We are forced to live life, not on the basis of our first choices, but on other choices. We are all forced to take less than what we wanted or less than what we designed. Accidents, death, reversal, failure will change our plans.

Amos consoles, "Don't worry about it, God is in it. God will see you through it. God is in the storm. God is in the heartaches. God is in the sadness. God is in the failure. God's activity is seen, and none of those things can take you away from the promises of God. Everything that God allows in your life, he allows for his loving purpose. It is hard to believe that God can love us that much. Nothing just happens. The hand of God directed it. How often we have gone through experiences frustrated and defeated. Yet in looking back on those experiences, we could say, "Now I can see the hand of God in it. He was there all the time. I just didn't see it." Here was a picture of a sovereign God working through the activities of his created universe.

Starting in verse 12 there is what I would call *accountability*. All of the things described in verses 6-11 were God's attempt to draw repentance from his people. Here was a paradox. There is the picture of a Sovereign God, a God who is ruler over the universe he created. But far from man's being a puppet in the hands of a God who gives no joy or responsibility to man, the message clearly comes back: God is sovereign in his activity, but man is accountable. You say, "I just can't accept man's responsibility and God's sovereignty." Now watch out! That's what liberals do. Anything they don't understand, they just don't accept. They explain it away. "It's impossible for an east wind to come up and split the waters. So, since I can't understand that, then I have to conclude that there was no splitting of the Red Sea, and there was no parting of the waters of Jordan. So I have to say that it didn't happen."

We will never fully understand the sovereignty of God and the responsibility of man, but they are both true. A sovereign God moves in the activity of nature in order to call responsible people to repentance. Certainly God could not condemn Israel if the people were not responsible for repentance. It was God's choice and not man's. So, beginning in verse 12, we read "Therefore, thus will I do unto thee, O Israel: and because I will do this unto thee, prepare to meet thy God." Man does have a responsibility under God. Don't wait for God to strike you down like he did Saul of Tarsus on the Damascus Road. When God moves in your heart and he speaks to you, it is God's way of saying, "Now you know. You are accountable for what you know." Five times in verses 6-11 is that haunting refrain, "Yet ye have not returned unto me, saith the Lord."

Oh, what a catalog of disaster. Famine. Drought. Scorching heat. Mildew. Locusts. Pestilence. Plagues. Wars. Natural disasters. Earthquakes. Volcanic eruptions. Yet God was still ignored. When you look at that, all that God has done and is doing, you realize how hard-hearted man is. What must God do to get our attention? What must he do to help you understand how much he loves you and wants to bless you? What's he going to do to America? Look at spiraling inflation that is far more than the reports indicate. Look at the disasters economically, morally, and spiritually that are coming upon this land. What must God do to get our attention. When will we recognize the hand of God in the affairs of men and our accountability unto him? He gave us prosperity and we didn't respond. He gave us peace and we didn't respond. And now we have come to a day when you and I will spend more time locked up in our houses than the criminals will in our prisons. The family is disintegrating before our eyes, and there is strong urging today to pass legislation that will let children, when they become teenagers, "divorce" their families. Courts in New York have already taken children out of Christian homes because the children complained, and the courts ruled that the parents had no right to bring them up as Christians. We are accountable. The sovereign God has designed the activities of this world to bring us to repentance.

Now, notice another fact of this accountability, and it is precious. God gave them one more chance. They didn't hear the moving in nature, so he sent them his prophet. God sent them Amos, and God preached to them through Amos. God through Amos told them, "How much I love you and how much I want you." It had life, it had meaning. Amos laid before them a fearful challenge, "Prepare to meet thy God." Amos studiously avoided pointing out Israel as a chosen, privileged people. He tried to let them know they were not God's pets. They had a responsibility. Here he broke his own rule that he had followed up to this point and cried prepare to meet *thy* God. *Thy* God. He is your God. He loves you, he has guided you, he has protected you. He has given you grace and mercy. He is your God, but prepare to meet him. They could prepare two ways. By repentance, they received God's pardon. By rejection, they received God's punishment. There was one last opportunity, a tremendous call to them and us from God.

Look at verse 13. It is what I call *acclamation*. I am convinced that we have too low a view of God. We have forgotten who God is. Here in verse 13 we have a portrait of absolute omnipotence, complete power. God formed the mountains, created the winds, declared the thoughts of men, made morning out of darkness, treaded the high places of the earth. He described a God who has power over everything visible. He formed the mountains with their majesty, their grandeur, the awe-inspiring presence of the mountains as they rise from the plains of the earth. God formed them. Praise God for he is the Creator of all that is visible.

More than that, he created the wind so he is sovereign, He also has power over the invisible, over that which is not seen with the eye, Over that vast world of human experience that cannot be described in terms of the material. He has power over the invisible.

More than that he has power even over the thoughts of men. He declares to man what his thought is. Even in the rationale of human intelligence God has power. He has power to transform, for he makes "the morning darkness." A better translation is "he makes morning out of darkness." He banishes the darkness with the brilliance and light of the sun. That is the God we serve. He has power to transform. He has power to change darkness into light. He is omnipotent, sovereign right here on this earth. We know he's sovereign in eternity, in heaven. The Word declares he's sovereign on earth. He is sovereign right here, not just on the streets of gold in the by and by, but on the dirty asphalt of the here and now—he is Lord! This verse ends with, "The Lord, The God of hosts, is his name."

The word for Lord here is Jehovah. It is the word given of the redeeming God, of the God who delivered them out of Egypt, the God who moved on a graceless and undeserving people and brought them out of slavery into the land of their inheritance. He is a redeeming God. He is the Lord. He is the covenant God. He is still that kind of God. This message is one of hope, reminding us that in every experience, there is the hand of God. In every sadness, heartache, and disappointment, there's the hand of God. You are not separated from him in the storm or in the failure. He is there. Grab his hand, turn to Him. Let every experience propel you to his presence!

9
Repentance or Disaster
(Amos 5:1-11)

Carefully read this pungent passage. Now as always Amos is strangely contemporary with us. He hits us where we live and in the day we live.

Throughout the Book, he has spoken of impending, imminent judgment upon the nation of Israel. He has warned the people that if they did not return to the Lord, there would be devastation upon the land.

In this passage, he sort of reversed the situation. Before this he had started out with the destruction that was coming and then preached, "If you will repent, you can avoid the consequences." Now he deals with judgment, destruction, and devastation *first*—in dramatic fashion. He came before the people and began a chant. It is called a lamentation here, but it was a funeral dirge. In Hebrew his chant was in meter and rhyme. Each line had three plus two beats—it was syncopated.

Imagine the effect on his listeners as they gathered to hear his sad lamentation, his woeful incantation. He preached their funeral while they were still alive. He warned of what God was about to do.

Notice this passage under three particular headings. First, *the destruction*. In verses 1 through 3, then in verse 6, and at the end of verse 11, let's see how he described their upcoming destruction. First, he chanted that "the virgin of Israel is fallen; she shall no more rise." Here, maybe for the first time, the nation of Israel was compared with a woman. This concept which God

gave to Amos and other Old Testament prophets perhaps
became the basis for the New Testament reminder that the
church is "the bride of Christ." We are spiritually in relationship
with him as a wife to a husband.

"The virgin of Israel has fallen." She had lost her purity and
ceased to be a virgin. She did so by an illicit love affair with
pagan gods, by turning away from the precepts and principles of
Jehovah God. The nation had gone away from Jehovah and his
teachings. They had compromised themselves, worshiping that
which was not God. Thus, he used the description of the fallen
virgin. "She shall no more rise." It was a picture of total
collapse—death where there should have been life. A young
woman should look forward to relations with her husband and
the procreation of a family. Here was one who would never know
that kind of relationship, for she had lost that purity and would
never recover from it.

Amos also described her as being "forsaken upon her land."
There were none to raise her up. There was isolation and
loneliness. "She is forsaken upon her land." What a tragic
statement concerning the evil consequences of sin and the effect
of judgment! That is what the Bible tells us. We may sin in a
group or as a nation, but we shall stand, one by one, all alone
before God. Though our sins may involve others, there will be
an awareness that we are utterly forsaken, unless we have
repented.

Then he launched into the physical destruction of the country. A city with a thousand would have only 100 left. A burg with
100 would have only ten. If my arithmetic is correct, that
constitutes a 90 percent loss. A decimation of the populace. The
cities, towns, and villages would be leveled. There would no
longer be productivity.

In the last portion of verse 11 he preached, "Ye have built
houses of hewn stone, but ye shall not dwell in them; Ye have
planted pleasant vineyards, but ye shall not drink of them." The

devastation was fearsome. In verse 6 there was the admonition: "Seek the Lord and ye shall live; lest he break out like fire in the house of Joseph." The mention of fire refers to the judgment of God which would come to remove evil so the good and the godly could prosper. Since most of the nation was involved in the sin, there would be precious few left.

Verse 6 speaks about the fire breaking out and devouring the nation, and there would be "none in Bethel to quench it." Their religious ceremonies and rituals would not be able to deliver them. The passage treats destruction, and then there is God's call to his people. God is always seeking, even though despair is in the air, even though it appears judgment is going to fall on the people. Still he cried (and cries today), "Seek the Lord, and ye shall live!"

Second of all there was *the distortion* we view in these verses. That God offered life to them was a redemptive fact, but the people distorted the truth of God through their hollow worship at their religious shrines. Amos declared on behalf of the Lord, "Don't seek me at Bethel. Don't seek me at Gilgal. Don't seek me at Beersheba." The people were shocked because these represented the most sacred places in the Northern Kingdom.

Do you remember what happened at Bethel? The patriarch Jacob came there twice. When he was fleeing his brother Esau, he came there at night to rest and made a rock for a pillow. As he slept that night he saw a ladder extended from earth to heaven. He beheld angels ascending and descending the ladder. You remember when he awakened he mused to himself, *Surely the Lord is in this place, and I knew it not.* When he came the first time to Bethel, he was a man with a past. When he left he was a man with a future. God had shown his divine blessings and unction. When he went the second time Jacob wrestled with the angelic messenger from God. He contended, "I will not let thee go until you bless me." He was smitten with a hip thrown out of joint and walked with a limp the rest of his life as a testimony of his struggle at Bethel. Out of it all God changed his name to Israel. He became the father in the line of Abraham. From him and his new name would proceed the very nation of Israel. But the prophet cautioned them, "Don't go to Bethel," even though it was perhaps the most hallowed of the shrines. Astounding!

Amos then referred to Beersheba. He also harked back to the patriarchs. Abraham, Isaac, and Jacob all three came to Beersheba, and there they heard God pledge his companionship to them. God assured those men, "I am with you," at Beersheba. So, Beersheba became a symbol of God's promise never to forsake or leave his people, but now the prophet warned, "Don't go to Beersheba." Amazing!

And Gilgal. After the Hebrews crossed the Jordan River going into Jericho, they camped the first night in Canaan—at Gilgal. There they erected a monument with twelve stones, reaffirming their covenant relationship with Jehovah. At Gilgal the manna stopped falling, and the people then ate the fruit of Canaan. At Gilgal they possessed the land which God had promised them. Gilgal was a sign of God's inheritance to them, a promise and fulfillment of all God had pledged to do. What a sacred place Gilgal was, but the prophet counseled, "Don't go to Gilgal." That would be like Christ saying, "Don't go to church."

The reason for the prohibition was: They had distorted the truth of God. These centers of worship had become compromised and perverted with agricultural pagan gods and the worship of that which was not God. The people had reached the pitiful place where they felt all they had to do was appear at a shrine. All they had to do was come to Bethel, Beersheba, or Gilgal, simply "punch the clock" down at the "church." Now the religious shrines had become hotbeds of sin and compromise. Then they thought God would be happy. They could live as they pleased and do as they wished. They came to church, sang, recited the Scriptures, worshiped of a sort, and went away unchanged, untouched. Their lives were unaltered by what they had done.

Verse 7 speaks about "ye who have turned judgment to wormwood." In other words, they had perverted justice. Justice was reserved only for the few. They had left off righteousness. They were "religious" people distorting the purpose of religion. They supposedly had come to worship God, but that God was lost in their deluge of religious formalism. They did everything that was appropriate to do. They went away unchanged, unmoved—and undone.

And there is such a distortion in our day. What difference does God make in our lives? I speak of ours collectively. Who is leading the fight for justice? Who is crying for compassion? Certainly not the religious people. We have become modern-day stoics. It is an affront to a Holy God for his people to claim, "I believe in God, but I want to do what God says only on Sundays," and we go through the motions and play church. There is no difference in us. And today people outside the church are not fighting the church—they are ignoring it. *You don't fight nothing*. You don't fight anything that is limpid, paltry, and puny. You fight intensity and aggressiveness. The church of the Lord Jesus Christ has largely become content to hide within its walls and pantomime its way through the rituals of faith. Christianity is not an addendum to life. It is life. It is the essence of it all.

The day is coming—and now is—when God is going to check us out. He is going to test what we believe. The time of pretending is gone. Our lack of concern is an insult to God; an accusation against the holiness of God; an affront to the Deity of God. It is an assault on the power of God; it is an insult to the presence of God for us to claim we know him and live like we do—unaffected, untouched, immobile. The sad fact is that we don't even do what the law requires. About all the American Christian does—and he doesn't do that too well—is attend. We don't tithe as we should. We don't give our time. We are a nation of spectators. The preaching hour has become a display, a show, a performance for the people in the pews to judge. We listen, then go home, and critique the sermon. We don't hear with the "ears" of our hearts. And that is a deadly distortion. God yearns for us to seek him, but we have forgotten who he is. God is not a moron who doesn't understand what is going on, but we treat him like that! They had distorted the worship of God because they did not know who he is.

"Seek him who maketh the seven stars and Orion." The stars in those days were believed to control the seasons, and so the prophet was speaking of the God who literally controlled the seasons and the universe itself. He is the God they were to seek. He is the God who turns "the shadow of death into morning." That phrase, "the shadow of death," is the same as used by the psalmist in Psalm 23: "Yea, though I walk through the valley of the shadow of death, I will fear no evil." It refers not merely to death itself, but to the deepest, darkest valleys one could imagine. The prophet advised the people, "You need to seek the One who alone can turn the deepest night into morning." Only God can do that! Seek him who has the reins of the universe in his hands. Amos was indicating, "God is the One who causes the night so you can rest.

Turn to the God who "maketh the day dark with night: that calleth for the waters of the sea, and poureth them out upon the face of the earth. The Lord is his name" (v. 8). He makes the day into night to give us respite from the glare and heat of the sun. That God "calleth for the waters of the sea, and poureth them out upon the face of the earth." There Amos had in mind the waters being drawn through evaporation out of bodies of water into the clouds and then ultimately restored to the earth through rain which replenished that earth. Only God can do that. They were to seek *The* Lord behind the universe—the Creator, the Sustainer, the Redeemer, and not the fictitious fertility gods and goddesses of surrounding cultures.

There was nothing wrong with the religious shrines within themselves. They were legitimate. Bethel seemed to symbolize abundant life. Beersheba represented God's presence and peace. Gilgal held the promise of security, God's giving our inheritance in him. And isn't that what Jesus offers us? Life. Peace. Security.

However, what Amos emphasized was: It is one matter to hear a promise but another to receive it. Amos's generation was not benefiting from the deeply spiritual meanings behind the shrines founded by their patriarchal predecessors. The pledges and promises of God were not "coffee-table" objects or brick-a-brack. They were not merely to be "ooohed" and "aahed" over, but were to be incorporated into people's lives.

God wanted to give comfort, life, and security to the Israelites. But going through the motions didn't make it.

Now we notice *the distinction*. Amos sort of approached this aspect from a side door and through contrast. Verse 10 says, "They hate him that rebuketh in the gate, and they abhor him that speaketh uprightly." The gist of this was that even the town leaders despised the man who would rebuke the community for their evil and would tell the truth, regardless of the consequences. They also hated God's prophet who preached an unpleasant message of rebuke and warning of retribution.

Contrary to those who "hate him that rebuketh" and "him that speaketh uprightly," the true believer loves the rebuke of evil and the telling of the truth. The genuine follower of God loves the voice of God's law.

Face it. You can recognize where you are spiritually by what you do with the principles of God's Word. We do much in our lives simply because God said we ought to do it, but we often fume and fuss if we are doing such from a sense of pressure or oughtness. The person who is always arguing with God's precepts is surely not committed to God. Full commitment means that we long to live by God's dictates. So, Amos had made a distinction.

Amos throughout his prophesy decries the false, the unreal, the hypocritical. If we could distil his preaching it would boil down to this: What good is your religion if you fail to put it into action? Today, probably more people are going to hell religiously than any other way. They are depending on ritual and formalism, as were the Israelites. The Ayatollah Khomeini is fanatically religious Muslim, but he has had multiplied thousands of his own people executed, including those who helped him rise to power. How well we remember his condoning the taking of American hostages. Religion. Religion. Done in the name of religion. Why do people who claim the name of Jesus Christ fight with and kill each other in Northern Ireland? Consider the recent massacre of Palestinians by so-called "Christian" Falangists in Beirut, Lebanon. The mass murder has caused an uproar around the world—and that murder was perpetrated under the name, "Christian." Think about all of the Americans who claim to be born again. Yet, where are the majority of them on a given Sunday? And they thin out even more on Sunday night and Wednesday night. Religion. Religion. The black spiritual goes, "Everybody talkin' 'bout heaven ain't goin' there." How can a person boast that he belongs to Christ and refuse to obey him?

A person told me the other day, "Well, I just worship God in my own way." You don't worship God in your own way. You worship God in *his* own way. Anything less is mere religion.

Let me nail down a peg here. The person who submits to the law of God is truly liberated. The person who defies that law is a slave. What a paradox! Jesus said, "The thief cometh not, but for to steal, and to kill, and destroy: I am come that they might have life, and that they might have it more abundantly." (John 10:10). There is a distinction when we truly follow Jesus Christ.

There is a second distinction in verse 11: "Forasmuch therefore as your treading is upon the poor, and ye take from him burdens of wheat. . . ." The Israelites were disregarding the rights of the downtrodden and poor, the disenfranchised. Greedy, politically powerful people oppressed the politically weak persons who had no one to speak for them—but God and his prophet. Throughout his message Amos contrasted these wicked, unscrupulous practices with godly actions and dealings. Here were blatant examples of rich Israelites cheating the poor Israelites. Face it. Hasn't this even happened among Christians today? How could a Christian employer mistreat his employers? How could a Christian employee not give his boss an honest day's work for an honest day's pay? Isn't it strange, too, that often the place we are most likely to be condemned is at church and that the most likely source of criticism is a fellow Christian? Doesn't make sense, does it?

I have spent nearly an hour with Madalyn Murray O'Hair and have found her to be much more gracious than some Baptists I know. Unusual, isn't it? And dreadfully convicting. If we are true believers, we ought to guard our fellowship. We should hurt with one another, laugh with one another, share with one another. We must stand together. There is no place for oppression in true New Testament churches. We've forgotten who the enemy is. He's Satan, the old devil—not our own brothers and sisters in Christ. If most Baptists would spend as much time witnessing to the lost as they do talking about one another, we could revolutionize our communities overnight. People who genuinely love the Lord guard the fellowship.

Throughout this passage there is the word *seek*. The prophet and other Old Testament writers employ that word, *seek*. I realize that there is a sense in which God is doing most of the seeking, and that he meets us more than halfway. You've heard the statement: "Religion is man seeking God. Christianity is God seeking man." God seeks. He initiates that seeking, but we are to respond and move toward him with all of our hearts. Seeking the Lord is serious, and it requires a definite decision. Seeking almost implies a groping in the dark. Seeking him may seem tedious for awhile—but remember that God is seeking, too. Through Christ we meet somewhere near the middle.

He has promised: If we seek we shall find. When you seek

with all of your heart, I guarantee that you'll find him, and he'll find you. Destruction is imminent, distortion is woven into religion and society, but there is the distinction of God's people who love his Word, guard his fellowship, and seek the Lord.

10
The Fruit of Repentance
(Amos 5:12-15)

Amos was one of the sternest Old Testament prophets, yet his message was tinctured with the grace of God. The people, however, refused to respond affirmatively.

First, I would have you look at *infinite knowledge.* "For I know your manifold transgressions and your mighty sins: they afflict the just, they take a bribe, and they turn aside from the poor in the gate from their right" (v. 12). Sometimes we answer "I know" when we don't. But God knows. God has perfect knowledge—omniscience. This theme runs throughout the Word of God.

In 1 Chronicles 29:17 God is described as One who "tries the reins" of the heart. All through the Psalms God is portrayed as searching and knowing us. "O Lord, thou hast searched me, and known me" (Ps. 139:1). In Jeremiah 11:20 is the same thought— he tries the reins of the heart. Jeremiah 17:10*a*: "I the Lord search the heart, I try the reins."

God is fully aware of everything in our lives. Even though he knows our hearts and minds, he still loves us. As humans we have the tendency to love those only with whom we agree—the people who please us and do what we want them to do. But God is vastly different. He loves us and is willing to redeem us, no matter how grossly evil and jaded we are. "But God commendeth his love toward us, in that while we were yet sinners, Christ died for us" (Rom. 5:8). The lovely truth running alongside his omniscience is his infinite love.

Transgression was a sin of rebellion. The word in Hebrew meant to "go across" something, to violate it, to break it. God knew how the people had violated his precepts and cut across the grain of his divine plan. He knew their "mighty sins." Their huge—to use a current expression, "humongous"—sins. And God can't be duped. You can't fool him. Somehow we return to the divine principle: "Be sure your sin will find you out." We can't pull the wool over God's eyes. "I know your manifold transgressions and your mighty sins."

"They afflict the just, they take a bribe, and they turn aside the poor in the gate from their right" (v. 12*b*). Their transgressions and sins were immediately linked to social injustices. Remember that a sin against man is ultimately a sin against God. The Psalmist cried, "Against thee, thee only (God), have I sinned." They punished the innocent. They rewarded the guilty. They cheated and conned. They had no concern for the downtrodden when they sought justice before the authorities.

Even today how often do we hear of an exceedingly wealthy person being sentenced to a long prison term, even for murder? When a man was innocent in those days he was often oppressed and sentenced. The guilty man would often bribe the judges and go free. When we sin against other people, we are sinning against God. Taking advantage, oppressing others, distorting the truth all are sins against man—but more so against God. This very idea was carried over into the teachings of Jesus. In his Olivet Discourse (Matthew 25:31-45) the major thrust centers around what humans have done to and for others. Jesus would declare to "the blessed of my Father" [the saved]: "Inherit the kingdom prepared for you from the foundation of the world: For I was an hungred, and ye gave me meat: I was thirsty, and ye gave me drink: I was a stranger, and ye took me in: Naked, and ye clothed me: I was sick and ye visited me: I was in prison, and ye came unto me. . . . Inasmuch as ye have done it unto one of the least of these my brethren, ye have done it unto me"

(25:34-36,40*b*). Our relationship to one another is a reflection of our relationship with God.

And God declared to the Israelites: "I know. . . ."

In verse 13 see the *inevitable result.* They lived with no thought toward God. They would reap the bitter harvest. "Therefore the prudent shall keep silence in that time; for it is an evil time." According to many commentators "the prudent" stands for those who wanted to succeed, who wanted to be accepted. In those days the man concerned about his self-interest kept his mouth shut. Why speak out? Don't get involved. Don't express your horror over what's going on. Don't rock the boat. Let sleeping dogs lie. We are living in a day of "peace at any price." Where are those who will stand up for what is right, what is proper, what is biblical? Where is the person who will cry out, "Even if my stand for Christ is unpopular, I'm going to be identified with him"? I pray that we will stop being Democrats or Republicans and just be Americans—and stand for the right, regardless of the party. The person who won't stand for something will fall for anything. When a country is steeped in manifold transgressions and mighty sins, people are afraid to "make waves." That had happened in Israel. The prudent kept silent.

Now, verses 14 and 15 speak of *individual obedience.* "Seek good, and not evil, that ye may live: and so the Lord, the God of hosts, shall be with you, as ye have spoken. Hate the evil, and love the good, and establish judgment in the gate: it may be that the Lord God of hosts will be gracious unto the remnant of Joseph." "Seek good," he counseled. There were positive and negative aspects. You seek good. In so doing you answer *no* to evil. When we seek good we are seeking God and what he wants. One primary truth of God's word is the goodness of God. God is good. He does right.

We must have a positive and negative side to our Christian life-styles. We Christians are often known as people who are "ag'in" things. Rather, we should be a people who are for something. If we stand unashamedly for the truth of God, the negatives will fall into place. Yes, we need to shun evil, but also to seek for the good and the right. The Bible emphatically teaches that we are to shun evil, that we are not to "give place to the devil," that we are to "flee youthful lusts," for instance. But it also admonishes us to: "Seek ye first the kingdom of God and his righteousness" (Matt. 6:33a).

Balance 14 and 15 and you'll notice that he asked them to seek good before they loved good. That's how we do it. We want to have "the feeling" before we act. Many people have remarked to me, "I want to be saved, but I don't feel it." What difference does that make? Feeling has nothing to do with it. How you feel is not significant. The important consideration is not your feelings but the fact that is associated with your experience. Amos taught, "Seek good"—then you'll love God and good. One writer has commented to me: "I hate to write; I love *having written*." That aptly expresses what I have in mind. In essence, Amos preached, "Do the right thing, and you'll love having done it." If you wait until you "feel like it," there'll be many things you'll never accomplish. Obedience simply means doing what God wants you to do, and after you've done that, you'll love having done it.

We seek the good and then we love the good. I love it because I do it. That's true of the entire Christian life. If I waited until I wanted to witness, I'd probably never do it. I do it because God says for me to do it. Having done it I'm glad I did. If I had waited until I could afford to tithe, I never would have done it. How you *feel* about doing the will of God is not the capstone. God said for us to do it. Our part is to do it. He'll bless us with feelings, emotions we ought to have, but we have to do it first. It's similar to taking medicine. When you become sick, you take your medicine, and then you feel better. You may not want to take your medicine, but you do it. After you do it, then the medicine is able to work, and you feel better. Spiritually the same fact is true. We seek good and then we love that good. We shun evil and then we hate evil. If I waited until I really hated my sins, I might never give them up. I might never turn them over to the Lord. I shun evil because God has commanded me to do it. The trouble with most American church members is that they are merely doing everything on the basis of how they feel. If they feel like doing it, they do it. If they don't feel like it, they don't do it. Yet, God has given us clear instructions in his Word about how to live and conduct ourselves.

The best advice anyone ever gave was Mary's suggestion to the stewards [servants] at the wedding feast in Cana of Galilee. "Whatsoever he (Jesus) saith unto you, do it" (John 2:5). If you wait until you want to do it, until you like doing it, until you love doing it, you'll never do it! Many people have fallen prey to the satanic lie, "Wait until you *feel* like it, until things are different." Satan wants you to wait, to put it off, to delay for the right feelings.

People are emotional. Feelings are important, but there are some things we should do, whether or not we feel like it. Having done it, you'll love it. You'll know you've done right, and God will bless you for it and in it.

Now notice: "Seek good, and not evil" (14*a*). "Hate the evil, and love the good" (15*a*). The promise of verse 14 is: "And so the Lord, the God of hosts, shall be with you, as ye have spoken." The promise of verse 15 is: "It may be that the Lord God of hosts will be gracious unto the remnant of Joseph." The phrase, "that ye may live," in 14 carries with it an imperative. *Live* is imperative. It is as though he wrote, "Seek good and not evil, and I command you to live." In other words, if you do that, it will be impossible for you not to live. It was a promise from God.

It is God's nature to give life. God is not a cosmic bluenose who enjoys taking all the fun and excitement out of life. God is the One who comes to give life! Jesus declared: "I am come that they might have life, and that they might have it more abundantly" (John 10:10). Life is the gift of God. The gift of eternal life he holds within himself. "And this is the record that God hath given to us eternal life, and this life is in his Son: he that hath the Son hath life, and he that hath not the Son of God hath not life" (1 John 5:12-13). Life is in God. God is life-giving and life-sustaining. It is also his nature to be gracious.

We have often overemphasized the love of God, and many people view God as though he would simply overlook our faults. There is an aspect of his judgment that Amos is talking about. God is a God of grace, but that grace would have no meaning without his corresponding wrath against unconfessed, unforgiven sin. His love would have no significance without his intense hatred of that which is wrong, unrighteous, and unjust. God hates that which is against mankind's purpose, destiny, nature, and well-being. He is a gracious God who loves to forgive. Whenever a person seeks God and obeys him, that person finds mercy and forgiveness. God longs to see you in perfect harmony with him. He wants you whole and complete.

Shortly before his death, Jesus stood on a hill overlooking Jerusalem, to this day called "The Holy City." He wept over that wayward city: "O Jerusalem, Jerusalem, how oft would I have gathered you unto myself . . . but ye would not." The city would not accept him. It is God's nature to gather you to himself, to forgive, to cleanse, to give life, abundance, joy, and peace. So he calls to us: "Seek me and you will live." God will be gracious unto you. God knows everything about you—every intent, every attitude, every thought, every action, no matter how well you have endeavored to camouflage them. How would you feel if all of your thoughts came out loud? You would be embarrassed, wouldn't you? But God knows. I would be embarrassed. How would you feel if you and your spouse were chewing each other out, and suddenly you realized I was standing there? Your faces would flush and you'd probably be nicer, wouldn't you? But Jesus is there all the time. He knows. He sees. Isn't it sad that we have more concern about our reputations among our friends and associates than we do toward God Almighty? Every sin, every iniquity, every transgression, every act of rebellion or disobedience is a stinging blow in the face of God.

Amos stressed that God knows. We may cover up our sins from friends, neighbors, loved ones, business and church associates—but we cannot hide them from God! The result of sin will be "an evil time," a wicked society, where even good people are afraid to speak up because of societal consequences they fear. It is absolutely amazing that God still loves and forgives, even though he knows!

11
The Dark "Day of the Lord"
(Amos 5:16-20)

Therefore the Lord, the God of hosts, the Lord, saith thus; Wailing shall be in all streets; and they shall say in all the highways, Alas! alas! and they shall call the husbandman to mourning, and such as are skilful of lamentation to wailing. And in all vineyards shall be wailing: for I will pass through thee, saith the Lord. Woe unto you that desire the day of the Lord! to what end is it for you? the day of the Lord is darkness, and not light. As if a man did flee from a lion, and a bear met him; or went into a house, and leaned his hand on the wall, and a serpent bit him. Shall not the day of the Lord be darkness, and not light? even very dark, and no brightness in it? (5:16-20)

Whenever we encounter the word *therefore* it links us with what has gone on before. It is almost redundant for me to remind you of Amos's central teaching—God's judgment upon Israel's sins. He had called them to repentance, but the rebellious Israelites were devoted to their hypocritical life-styles. Throughout Amos 4 there was the recurring phrase, "yet have ye not returned unto me." In chapter 5 Amos had already pled with them three times to seek the Lord. "Seek ye me" (v. 4). "Seek the Lord, and ye shall live" (v. 6). "Seek him that maketh the seven stars and Orion" (v. 8). Amos had given them more than ample opportunity to seek the Lord and repent of their sins.

The deepest tragedy is: Even though God offered them life, he knew that the majority would reject him. Later on Amos would refer to a tiny remnant of true worshipers, but even they would suffer because of Israel's sin. Amos foresaw the dreadful "day of the Lord," a fiery judgment on the nation.

Three main thoughts are here. First is *authority*. Amos speaks of a God of omnipotence and sovereignty. He repeats the name Lord. "The Lord, the God of hosts, the Lord." The Lord spoke of God's eternal, never-ending providence and rulership—He is a God who does not change. Within these names of God are a treasury of concepts. God's veracity. When God makes a promise he carries it out. He makes no idle threats. When God makes a prophecy, rest assured that it will come to pass. The Lord of hosts means that he has authority over the host (the multitude) of heaven, earth, and the universe. There is also the idea that he is the leader of an innumerable army. He has generalship. He is the commander in chief of all the universe.

Most of us have a watered-down concept of God's power. God can do what he pleases, but it will always be right. He says what he means and means what he says. God never reneges on his promises. A promise of God is simply an established fact that God already sees as being realized. He looks at all eternity in one glance! Prophecy, which is God's promise to fulfill his Word, is merely history God has seen even before it happens. It is in the future tense for us—in the past tense for God. So, this passage reminds us of God's authority.

"Wailing" indicates the anguish, horror, suffering, and dismay which would befall the people on "the day of the Lord." Remember Jesus' statement about "weeping and wailing and gnashing of teeth." Verse 17 speaks about God passing through the midst of the people. Perhaps the people thought back to Egypt and the Passover. They heard their grandfathers and fathers talk about their forefathers' deliverance through Moses. God was going to pass through Egypt in retribution, but he would pass *over* those who followed his instructions about the blood being sprinkled over and around their doors. Every first-born son of Egypt died as the death angel passed through Egypt.

But he passed over the Hebrews' homes. Now, though, it appears that God is going to pass *through* Israel—not over them.

My, we Baptists and other evangelicals are always talking about revival and a visitation from God. The truth is: I am not sure most of us could handle a real, heaven-sent revival and visitation of God. If the presence and power of the Lord were manifested, they would burn away the dross of our sin. It would not be a joyful experience until it was over. When God passes through it is different from his passing over. Listen—when God passes through everything contrary to his nature is removed. Everything against his will is stripped away. So many talk about brokenness as if it were a Pollyanna experience. Brokenness before God is absolutely devastating. God declared, "I am going to pass through you."

In verse 18 Amos introduced the day of the Lord. The prevailing idea in Israel was: The day of the Lord was a time when God's judgment would fall on other nations on behalf of Israel. Israel would be liberated from the heathen peoples who afflicted her and would reign and rule supreme, becoming the dominant political force in the world. The concept of the coming day of the Lord was celebrated in many of their feasts and festivals. But Amos dashed their notions to pieces. Amos's slant was picked up by other prophets of that period such as Isaiah. Amos preached, "Yes, the day of the Lord is coming, but the judgment is going to fall on you, Israel." Only a morally righteous nation is going to rejoice over the day of the Lord. Israel didn't fill that bill. Only those who have been unjustly oppressed will be delivered in the day of the Lord.

Today we must understand the coming of the Lord into our lives. We have failed to realize that the way of life is through death. The way to comfort is through travail. Peter wrote that Jesus was "made perfect through sufferings." Our Lord didn't take the easy road. Coming to God is not a glib, giddy experience. It is a sobering time of reflection where we face the truth about ourselves. We live in the day of the dry eye unless we're crying over a silly movie, television play, or our financial setbacks. How many people are truly repentant and grieving over their sins against God? God is not an errand boy jumping at the chance to forgive our same sins over and over and over again. We don't know what repentance means. It means to hate our sins and to turn totally away from them. We counsel too many people who are not really willing to give up what stands between them and God. When you really repent, you're afraid to hold onto your sins. We talk people into an easy kind of commitment which calls for nothing but signing a decision card. Genuine, deep-down repentance and Bible-based faith are the answers.

Amos was trying to teach Israel an object lesson. I'll never forget preaching an eighteen-month-old girl's funeral. Ah, it was sad. The father's grief was doubly real because he had accidentally struck down and killed his precious child. He not only lost a daughter he loved—but he did it. You'd better not come to God with any less a sense of condemnation.

Amos pronounced a woe upon those who desired the day of the Lord. Why? Because the carnage and plunder of that day would be turned on them. He then painted the picture of anguish, wailing, and funeral lamentations in every place. He had in mind that they would even call the professional mourners, which was often the custom in those days. Those paid actors knew how to scream, sob, squeal, moan, and weep uncontrollably. They cried those huge crocodile tears. They even called the farmers to help out. The disaster and death would be so ghastly that they would have to enlist everybody to wail over the dark day of the Lord. Vineyards were normally festive places where there was celebration and singing. But even there would be lamentation. Hear me. Unless you come to God in repentance, there won't be enough people to wail for you during the day of judgment.

Verses 18 and 20 speak about the day of the Lord as being

"darkness and not light." The people previously thought it was light and glory for Israel. Verse 19 delved into the predicament which they would face. People would flee from one calamity only to fall headlong into another. Think of the poor guy running from a lion and falling into the clutches of a giant bear, or the fellow who ran into a house for refuge, leaned on a wall for momentary rest, and had a snake bite him. That meant the people could not escape God's wrath, no matter what they did. There is a contrast between darkness and light. Darkness refers to evil, oppression, failure, despair. Light symbolizes truth, success, joyfulness, happy experiences, buoyant spirits. The people of Israel thought the day of the Lord would be a bright, happy celebration for them. Instead it would be a time of unprecedented despair and dismal conditions. Israel had thought they were especially blessed of God because they had enjoyed prosperity. They had flourished materially with houses of ivory and splendid furnishings.

If I were to ask you, "How do you know God has blessed America?" what would you answer? Most people reply, "Why, it's plain. Look at the evidences of God's blessings. Food. A place to live. Freedom. A car. Television." That's what most people call blessings. Many people pray for revival in America because they think it will guarantee material blessings. As I write this the economy is sagging. We are in the worst recession since the Depression which started in 1929 and really ended at the outset of World War II. If God does not pass through America, we could lose everything. How can we pray for starving people when we have never suffered the pangs of extreme hunger? We've never seen our babies' stomachs distended from malnutrition.

Somehow we have the idea that blessing from God is synonymous with food and freedom, when in reality the severest danger in our lives is exactly that—the things which make us comfortable. You see, Amos's concept was a reversal of their expectations. They had expected that the day of the Lord would mean material superabundance, political power, and freedom for themselves. Yet, God showed Israel that their sins were even more grievous than those of the heathen, because Israel was God's chosen people. Yet, they had rebelled against and rejected him.

We Christians no longer believe it "is a fearful thing to fall into the hands of a living God." We are comfortable and complacent, and we are victimized by it. The day of the Lord is coming. It will be darkness and not light. This judgment is inescapable unless there is a wide-scale turning to God. But many Christians have become numb with this kind of message, exactly as Israel did. They want God's divinely called preacher-prophets to "shut up." But the Lord of hosts is not going to tolerate the gross evil of our nation and our lives.

Many of us are thinking, almost like the Israelites, *Ah, we're a good Christian nation. Look at all the other countries we've helped. God's going to punish wicked, atheistic Russia or Red China. But not us.* What's to exempt the United States? The day of the Lord may not be what we really want.

Yes, we ought to pray for revival and for the mighty movement of God's Spirit upon America. Yet, if God passes through, it will be disturbing and disruptive to us. He will sweep away everything contrary to his holiness. Right now we ought to petition the Lord of hosts: "Lord, what's your will for my life, no matter what it involves? Lord, take away everything in my life which displeases you. Lord, let me have wholeness and joy that a walk with you reveals."

12
Vain Worship
(Amos 5:21-27)

After preaching about the dark day of the Lord, Amos lashed out against their insincere worship. God was speaking through Amos as though he and the prophet were synonymous. The address was in the first person.

Verse 21: "I hate, I despise your feast days, and I will not smell in your solemn assemblies." "Smell" implies that God would not approve the odor of their burnt offerings. Verse 22 continued the theme, "Though ye offer me burnt offerings and your meat offerings, I will not accept them: neither will I regard the peace offerings of your fat beasts." Because of their sinful motives, injustice, and rebellion, their worship was an abomination to the Lord.

The passage is sobering, the setting simple. Both the religious leaders and the rank and file of the people thought they could obtain the favor of God by meticulous observation of religious rites and all the outward trappings of religion. They had perverted religion until they felt that the essential was going to church and taking a bow.

"I hate" was a severely strong word. God hated their feast days and all their fancy rituals, and their worship was unacceptable to him. "I will not accept them: neither will I regard the peace offerings of your fat beasts" (v. 22). He rejected their music: "Take thou away from me the noise of thy songs; for I will not hear the melody of thy viols" (v. 23). You could not find a more vivid description of divine displeasure outside of Revelation 3:16 where God said "I will spue [spit] thee out of my mouth."

Now notice *divine rejection*. Verses 21-23 emphasize that God rejected their worship. The people were faithful in carrying out religious rituals. When they did what they thought was a religious obligation, it was a sin. If that's true, then it perhaps means that in certain cases it is a sin to attend church. Imagine it. What God desired was more than the mechanics. He wanted creatures other than angels when he created man. The angels did God's bidding and were obedient. In man God created a rational mind and an ability to comprehend—with the faculty of responding to God. God wants a wholehearted response, not a plastic, going-through-the-motions one.

Notice how many times the second person possessive pronoun occurs. *Your* feast days, *your solemn* assemblies, *your* fat beasts, *your* songs, and *your* vials. When we pervert and twist what God has given us he disassociates himself from it. Don't blame God with it. It's our idea. We leave God out and then try to implicate him, but that is not going to work. What God desires from us is a sacrificial life and not an empty sacrifice. God wants people through which his Spirit can flow, not robots with mechanical adherence to ceremony and ritual.

He despised their feast days, and yet the people were expected to go. It was an obligation. God would have none of it. The Hebrews were highly developed with their music. They had chanters and singers—maybe even choirs. They used all types of instruments—stringed, percussion, and even wind instruments. To God it was noise. The kind of harmony God accepts goes beyond counterpoint, harmony, and decibels. God was sorely displeased with their services.

That thought is rather scary. How like the Israelites we are! Do you realize how much we take for granted? We as Christians sing all kinds of hypocrisies. "I Am Thine, O Lord." Are you? "I'll Go Where You Want Me to Go?" Really? Will you? I am fully convinced that many people do not sing in church, not simply because they have bad voices, but because they feel condemned and frustrated as they sing the words. Why do you go to church? Except for the habit of it and for an opportunity to show off, most of the Israelites had forgotten why they attended worship. If our lives are not into worship, if we are not obedient, if we are not in love with Christ, God hates our efforts. *Divine rejection!*

In verse 24 he starts out with a preposition—"But." That conjunction was divinely inspired, of course. The Lord was indicating that somehow they could turn around their unacceptable worship. *But* what? *Divine righteousness.* "But let judgment run down as waters, and righteousness as a mighty stream." To paraphrase it, "People, it's not too late. You let the judgment of God course through the land. Let righteousness come through like a rushing stream." They could do it. "Run down as waters" indicates abundance and perpetuity. Following God is neither a one-day-a-week pursuit nor a one-time experience.

Then we see *divine retribution.* God was at worship with them. Through Amos, God asked, "Have you offered unto me sacrifices and offerings in the wilderness forty years, O house of Israel?" Of course they did. Wherever Amos asked that question I am sure people nodded, answered yes, or even yelled the equivalent of amen. There was a hook in the question. The implication was they did offer to him in the wilderness, but there was more than that. God thought the people had committed themselves to him, not merely to sacrifices and offerings. He pointed out that ceremonial religion could keep people away from the truth and even be divorced from God's Word. That had happened in Israel.

"But ye have borne the tabernacle of your Moloch and Chiun your images, the star of your God, which ye made to yourselves." They had even mixed the worship of false gods with theirs. They had dabbled in the occult and had tried to form a syncretistic religion, combining Jehovah worship with the elements they picked up from ungodly fertility cults around them. Those very Israelites are now revealed as worshipers of pagan gods! On the surface they were supposedly sold out to the Lord of hosts, but he wasn't enough for them. They had a religious experience isolated from the Word of God.

Let me relate their idolatry to our day. There is plenty in worship today parading under the guise of Christianity. The only way to hold yourself in the mainstream is to rely on God's Word. Either the Bible is the Word of God or the word of mortal man. Men were used to record it, but they spoke the Word of God. We either accept it as the Word, sailing under its flag, or we drift into all kinds of perversity. Not long ago a church had to withdraw fellowship from a mother and her grown daughter who were reading palms and using crystal balls. Both of them testified, "God told us to do it." And this type of activity is going on all over in the name of Christianity. What is your basis? What is your mooring? God declared to Israel that they had none. "You are not only going through the motions down at the shrine, but you're having an affair with false gods and goddesses on the side," Amos accused. They had made images of false gods and perhaps even carried them in the processions leading to Bethel, Beersheba, and Gilgal. No doubt they were dabbling in astrology because those false gods were linked with particular stars—"the star of your god."

They had reached an abysmal state. Then God "let the hammer down": "Therefore will I cause you to go into captivity beyond Damascus, saith the Lord, whose name is the God of hosts" (v. 27). In their rebellion they had ended up fighting God himself. God implied that there was no sense in their arguing or fighting with him. Captivity was coming. God forbid it, but there could come a time when, in seeking to defend America, we could be fighting against God! What did he mean "beyond Damascus"? Because the gods mentioned in verse 26 were worshiped in the lands beyond Damascus, God was saying, "I am going to put your bodies where your hearts and minds have really been. I am sending you where they worship these pitiful, wicked gods all the time, not just part-time like you worship them." That frightens me.

Strange, but the Communists believe and practice an ideology most Americans believe but won't admit. Most Americans claim to believe in God but live as though he doesn't exist. We are practical atheists. We give lip service to God so long as it doesn't interfere with our idolatry. We are supposed to believe in God and trust him, but we don't obey him. God will tolerate our idolatry so long and perhaps say, "OK, if that's what you really believe, I'll let you live where they believe like you."

Unless there is a change, Christianity as we know it in America cannot meet its challenges. Our Christian forces are fragmented and immobile. Most of our membership is AWOL—absent without order of leave. Most of the soldiers are undisciplined and untrained. We have a whole lot of chiefs but very few Indians.

God says, "I'm going to win, and I'd like for you to be with me." God's sovereign purposes have not been detoured. History is still moving toward the climax when Jesus Christ will return and the kingdom of God will be established upon this earth; and he shall reign for ever and ever. Those who have committed themselves to him will reign with him.

Now notice how Amos concludes this compelling message. "Saith the Lord, whose name is The God of hosts." He is The God over against the false gods of Moloch and Chiun and thousands of other idols of mud, sticks, stones, houses, lands, bank accounts, and other objects. That Omnipotent God has spoken. Hear him now!

13
The Lap of Luxury
(Amos 6:1-6)

Bear in mind that Amos tears into hypocrisy with a vengeance. The last verse of the fifth chapter has dealt with Israel's formalistic, ritualistic worship without heart and deep commitment. Amos 6:1-6 is couched in terms of a religious ceremony and in the context of the liturgy. Amid that setting Amos preached, "Woe to them that are at ease in Zion, and trust in the mountain of Samaria, which are named chief of the nations, to whom the house of Israel came!" Zion was the holy mountain in Jerusalem of Judah, and the mountain of Samaria referred to Gerizim in Israel.

Peace and ease in the proper context are OK. Psalm 25:13, for instance, climaxes with the phrase, "his soul shall dwell at ease." Ease in that case was a promise of God, but here Amos did not have that kind of ease in mind. The "ease" of Israel was a carnal, ungodly ease. Amos portrayed people at ease when God was ill-at-ease over their sins. Israel was approaching life in a careless, casual, flippant manner when God desired genuine commitment and concern.

This passage reminds us of the seriousness of religious error and falsehood. Ritual and ceremony had become all the rage with them. That actually was the basis of error. More times than not, error springs from taking part of the truth and preaching it as though it were the *whole truth*—for instance, preaching the love of God to the exclusion of God's justice and righteousness. Error is seldom so far off base that it is easily detected. It can happen by taking a "text" and ignoring the "context."

There was nothing wrong with the original ceremonies and rituals set up in the Hebrews' worship—but the Israelites had isolated those worship symbols and made them ends in themselves. Worship ought always to involve an in-depth encounter with God Almighty; all we do should lead us into the presence of the Lord. They had missed the entire point of worship. The very things which should have brought them into a closer walk with God led them away from him. Somehow they had divorced their religious observations from morality and ethical principles. It was enough for them to go through the motions and to give verbal obeisance to God. The day following the worship service it was the status quo all over again. Lie. Cheat in business. Oppress the poor. Look down one's nose at others. There was no difference within their lives.

Mere religion cannot change lives. Observe Northern Ireland. Both sides are staunchly religious—the Protestants and the Catholics. Even the secret agents of the IRA claim to be devoutly religious. Iran is fanatically religious. The Ayatollah Khomeini is equivalent to a high priest. Religion doesn't provide the answer. Here in our country, religion is not answering our dilemmas. We are being overwhelmed by secular humanism that has not merely isolated itself within secular circles but has pervaded theology, education, and other aspects of life. Religion is not the answer, particularly when you set aside certain facets and cling to them as if they were the whole truth.

Now scan this passage with me. If one word could sum up verses 1 and 2 it would be *insolence*. They trusted in themselves and their religion. Their religion was not according to God's dictates. They fashioned religion from their own warped sense of values. The cities mentioned in verse 2 were examples of those which rejected God. Amos had no confidence in the privilege of being "the elect" claimed by a self-righteous nation whose life was not distinguishable from the so-called heathen around them. In other words, are you better than those cities you consider ungodly and corrupt? God's answer was a resounding no!

We must exercise care that we don't adopt an insolence about our nation. We are furiously competing with the Russians and Red Chinese in the building up of armaments. At the same time we are keeping them afloat with our shipments of foodstuffs and technology. We are trying to keep an international balance of power. And we are trusting in our institutions to save us. Many of you who read these pages believe that severe judgment could never fall on the United States. The history of Israel should cause us to tremble. Multiplied millions of God's "chosen people," the Israelites, have died at the hands of nations like the Babylonians, the Assyrians, and the Romans. The Muslims, as they swept across North Africa and Southern Europe under their early caliphs, slaughtered thousands of Jews. The macabre Inquisition, carried out in the name of religion, was responsible for other thousands of Jewish deaths. Persecution has continued throughout the centuries. Who could forget the Nazi purges of Jews under Hitler? At least six million died during his regime. Places like Belsen, Buchenwald, Ravenhorst, and Auschwitz stand as horrid, mute testimony to the extermination of the Jews. Stalin and other Soviet leaders conducted pogroms against the Jews. It's strange how Russian slaughter of the Jews has been brushed aside. It is estimated that about six million Jews died in Russian death camps during the 1920s, 1930s, and later. And we in the United States claim that God won't let anything happen to us!

God will not allow us to treat his worship with insolence and disregard as though his precepts do not matter. We act as though he has no rights. Some of us seem to preach that after you're saved, you have all kinds of options. You can join the church or not, be baptized or not, be active or not. Those are not options. It's time we stood up and were counted for the Lord. You see, though, we resist the purposes of God because of our insolence and pride.

Verse 3 explains their *indolence*. They wanted to rid their minds of thoughts concerning judgment. Many people act as if they are never going to die. They push the thought of hell, condemnation, and judgment back into their subconscious minds. The Israelites lived as though there were no eternity and no God. Listen, if we knew that Jesus were coming back today, we'd do differently, wouldn't we? But we don't know. We treat with disdain and half-heartedness the claims of God. "Ye that put away the evil day, and cause the seat of violence to come near." The seat of violence speaks about the leadership that people tolerate when their motivations become perverted. The people put up with wickedness in their leaders because they themselves were wicked. The British parliamentarian, Edmund Burke, declared: "All that is necessary for the triumph of evil is that good men do nothing." Push away God and thoughts of him. The process will submerge our nation. Discord will grow without being actively sown and cultivated. Evil will flourish. You don't have to grow weeds in a garden. They grow themselves. You don't have to sow seeds to wreck your marriage. Simply leave it alone. Neglect your mate and children. You don't have to abuse your children to destroy them. Just leave them alone. Few churches, beloved, are destroyed by acts of dissension. We simply ignore our responsibilities.

Indulgence sums up verses 4-6. There's a portrait of laziness, idleness, sensuality without the slightest hint of spirituality. Amos was not condemning those with material possessions. The Scriptures present two thoughts about material possessions. 1. We ought to gain them honestly and rightfully. 2. We ought not to abuse and misuse those possessions. The richness in Israel not only was languid and lazy but was also lawless. Amos had made it manifestly clear that oppression of others to get ahead was an earmark of the Israelites. They coveted. They cheated.

They stole. Amos condemned their opulence because of how they achieved it and how they used it.

We can honor or dishonor God with our possessions. When you come down to it, nothing really belongs to us. God owns 100 percent of it. My money, my time, my energy, my talents, my possessions, my very life belong to God. They misused their ill-gotten gains. Their beds were made of highly expensive ivory from elephants' tusks. They lay around on couches. They killed and ate animals prematurely, when they were not yet ready for the slaughter. They surrounded themselves with all kinds of musical instruments "like David." Sounds familiar, doesn't it? They had to be entertained constantly. They were not content to drink wine in cups. They had to have big bowls. They perfumed and powdered themselves to a fare-you-well. And they didn't care about the sickness of sin permeating Joseph. The age of Jeroboam II has been called "The Ivory Age." There is also the possibility that these bowls were dedicated vessels they might have purloined from a place of worship. In Exodus 27:3, 1 Kings 7:40, and 2 Kings 12:13 there are references to the making of bowls from precious metals. Amos may have condemned them not only for excessive drinking and drunkenness, but also for using sacred vessels as did Belshazzar at his drunken feast in Daniel 5.

Theirs not only was the sin of sensuality but of sacrilege and blasphemy—using the things of God for ungodly purposes. Could we do that today? Could a businessman use his church for gain? Or could a preacher be guilty? Or hide behind the church for a facade of respectability? The wrong use of the church or worship can become a means of soothing our consciences or even selfish indulgence.

The latter part of verse 6 reveals their utter indifference and insensitivity; they were "not grieved for the affliction of Joseph." Joseph refers to the many descendants of that patriarch, especially the tribes of Ephraim and Manasseh. The populace simply did not care. It was oblivious to the suffering in the land and unwilling to face the judgment which was pronounced by Amos.

Many of us are indifferent to the conditions around us. Instead of just railing against the sins around us, why not witness to the sinners? Why not reach the prostitute, the dope dealer, the purveyor of pornography. Put them out of business by reaching them for Christ Jesus. Precious few of us take seriously Jesus' call to pick up his cross and follow him daily. We are staring a complex situation in the face. We have become slaves in our own society. Inflation and recession have hit us. Millions are out of work. Other millions don't want to work. Crime has soared. Incurable herpes is on the rampage. Can we sit by and let the rest of the nation and world go to hell?

Only Christ can heal our nation, mend our marriages, restore our minds. Only he can soothe the broken-hearted and liberate us from the enslavement of sin. He's the One to whom we must turn. We must not be indifferent. Dear Lord, help us to be grieved for our world. "Blessed are they that mourn for they shall be comforted" (Matt. 5:4). Grieve not in despair but grieve with action. In giving comfort through Christ we may then be comforted.

I love the words of Adoniram Judson, "The future is as bright as the promises of God." In Christ it is. He is still in control. God help us to be driven to him—and not to be "at ease in Zion!"

14
Impending Judgment
(Amos 6:7-14)

Amos may remind us of a broken record played for God. The prophet was compelled, obsessed. He kept hammering away at the same nail. Through the Spirit's unction he reiterated the theme of impending judgment. Verse 6 which begins, "Therefore now shall they go captive with the first that go captive," refers back to the preceding six verses which began, "Woe to them that are at ease in Zion, and trust in the mountain of Samaria. . . . "

He had in mind those leading citizens who pampered themselves with luxury and a sensuous life-style. Those who led the people in sin would be the first to fall under captivity. Verse 8 is one of several places in Amos where God makes a solemn vow. "The Lord God hath sworn by himself, saith the Lord God of hosts, I hate the excellency of Jacob, and hate his palaces; therefore will I deliver up the city with all that is therein." God stressed that he was sick of their behavior. He abhorred and hated Israel's dishonest, selfish opulence—the nation's uppity style and mock elegance.

His prophecy revolved around the coming judgment and the fact that their sins were tightening the hangman's noose around their necks. Verses 7 and 8 speak of their arrogance and pride. In sinful pride the people had rejected God. No one would resist God were it not for the pride that swells up within one's heart.

Isaiah the prophet wrote about the fall of Satan, the devil, who is called "Lucifer, the son of the morning." "How art thou fallen from heaven, O Lucifer, son of the morning! how art thou cut down to the ground, which didst weaken the nations! (Isa. 14:12). How did sin start? "For thou hast said in thine heart, I will ascend into heaven, I will exalt my throne above the stars of God: I will sit also upon the mount of the congregation, in the sides of the north: I will ascend above the heights of the clouds; I will be like the most High" (Isa. 14:13-14). Lucifer fell because of his pride, and all sinners have followed the same pathway. Proverbs lists seven things the Lord hates. Among those are "a proud look."

The proud person puts himself and his own pleasures first. This passage of Scripture in Amos exposes the prideful people. Their greed was closely linked with their pride. Sensuality was too. Amos pinpointed their sin specifically. In this case "excellency" was pride. God hated what they did through their own power and pride. God hates pride because it hurts us. God wants what is best for us. He wants us to be joyful and fulfilled. God realizes that man, pursuing his wishes in his own energy, can never have joy and peace within.

Some translators render palaces as *citadels*. Perhaps God was thinking of their fortresses. They were trusting in human defenses rather than God who is our refuge and strength. They had used their fortifications as an excuse to leave God out of their lives. Does that sound familiar? Americans believe in themselves to the extent that you often hear this expression, "When there's a crisis, Americans will respond. They'll take a stand. They all sacrifice." We have become a self-sufficient nation. All of those civilizations which reigned fell—Egypt, Babylon, Syria, Assyria, Persia (now Iran), Greece, and Rome. To moderns *The Decline and Fall of the Roman Empire* may seem dull reading, but Gibbon, the historian, wrote an eye-opener. We in America are guilty of every sin the Romans committed: pleasure, greed, lust, dependence on the military, self-satisfaction, a pervading materialism, and a disregard for human personhood.

Israel later fell like a ton of bricks as Amos had prophesied. God swore according to his name. His conviction was so strong that he made a solemn oath upon his own name which is synonymous with truth. That was how desperately God hated pride.

Look at these Scriptures concerning pride.

Only by pride cometh contention: but with the well advised is wisdom (Prov. 13:10).

Every one that is proud in heart is an abomination to the Lord: though hand join in hand, he shall not be unpunished (Prov. 16:5).

Pride goeth before destruction, and an haughty spirit before the fall (Prov. 16:18).

Who have said, With our tongue will we prevail; our lips are our own: who is Lord over us? (Ps. 12:4).

The ultimate objective of pride is to rebel against God, to resist God. That causes us to feel, "I'm the ruler of my life." Or as William Ernest Henley put it: "I am the master of my fate. I am the captain of my soul." Such pride keeps the unsaved from salvation and the saved from a deep, satisfying experience with the Lord.

Read Psalm 52:7: "Lo, this is the man that made not God his strength; but trusted in the abundance of his riches, and strengthened himself in his wickedness." The Israelites were trusting in their riches. They had fallen into the entrenchment of evil. Job 21:22: "Shall any teach God knowledge? seeing he judgeth those that are high." In other words, who can teach God anything? Yet pride tries to do exactly that. "Listen, God, I know a whole lot about this situation. I can't accept what you're teaching. In my case it's different." And we also try to instruct

God in our prayers. I've heard people try to do it publicly. "Now, listen God. We know what's best. We're so good, and we're getting better all the time." They may not pray in exactly those words, but you sense it in the tenor of their prayers. We don't need to teach God. We need to learn from him and agree with him. The proud heart tries to tell God what is best, as if he were pitifully ignorant and woefully unlearned.

Turn to Job 40:11-12. Verse 11 teaches that the proud are to be brought down low, and 13 continues that theme. "Hide them in the dust together." The prideful person deserves to eat the dust and wallow in it. Jesus taught that the person who exalts himself shall be abased [brought low, brought down] and the person who humbles himself shall be exalted (see Luke 14:11). First Peter 5:5 intreats the younger to respect their elders and "to be clothed with humility; for God resisteth the proud, and giveth grace to the humble."

Arrogance and pride were at the root of Israel's sin. You and I will also have to deal with it in our lives. Our questioning of God and resisting his will stem from pride. No one really wants to admit that he is dependent, that he is inadequate, that he cannot measure up by himself.

Verses 9-14 foretell the doom to fall upon them. It would be a widespread destruction—"from Hemath unto the river of the wilderness" (v. 14). That's similar to our saying from the Atlantic to the Pacific, from the Gulf of Mexico to Canada. Let the phrase, "The Lord commandeth," grab you. In the Old Testament there was the concept concerning direct causation. The prophets viewed Israel's history, whether victorious or disastrous, as the direct intervention of God. For instance, in Psalm 148:5 there is the same expression: "Let them praise the name of the Lord: for he commanded, and they were created." God commanded. Creation came at the command of God. "Let there be light." "Let there be a firmament in the midst of the waters, and let it divide the waters from the waters." "Let the" and "let there be" in Genesis 1 were the commands of God in creation. When God commands creation, creation is accomplished. When God commands destruction, it comes to pass.

In verse 11 there is the smiting of "the great house with breaches, and the little house with clefts," meaning that God was going to include the big shots and the little ones as well, the leaders and the followers. If the smile of God is upon a leader, blessings flow upon his people. If a leader sins against God, his people suffer because of his warped judgment and faulty decisions. We should bombard heaven on behalf of our leaders—mayors, governors, congressmen, senators, state assembly members, the president of the United States and his cabinet.

In verses 12 and 13 he notes a paradox. "Shall horses run upon a rock? will one plow there with oxen?" (v. 12*a*). Amos asked these questions with intent because it was not customary for horses to run upon a rock. He may have envisioned a rocky cliff or incline which would have impeded the running of horses. How could you plow with oxen on a rocky cliff face? Some translators have felt the passage should be rendered "plow the sea," making it a genuine impossibility. And yet, the prophet cried, "ye have turned judgment into gall, and the fruit of righteousness into hemlock." Even though horses and oxen would find it nigh onto impossible to run or plow on rocks or the sea, the Israelites had turned judgment and righteousness into bitter potions and poisons! They had contradicted every law of God. They had perverted and twisted God's intentions and attributes.

Verse 13 is rendered in *The New American Standard Bible*: "You who rejoice in Lodebar, And say, 'Have we not by our own strength taken Karnaim for ourselves?'" Lodebar literally means "a thing of nothing" or just "nothing." Karnaim means "a pair of horns." Lodebar and Karnaim were towns nearby, so whatever the meaning, the text implies that the people were bragging on the king for capturing a couple of towns, when it meant nothing in the sight of God. God was declaring, "You rejoice over what doesn't matter, yet you corrupt everything. You have poisoned a meaningful society until there are no judgment and righteousness left. They had sinned heinously, yet they were supposed to be God's people. God's people ought to be different, but Israel wasn't. The Israelites rejoiced in "Lodebar" ("a thing of nought" or "nothing").

By this time I assume that many of the unbelievers had become "believers," even though they perhaps did nothing about it. Verse 14: "But, behold, I will raise up against you a nation, O house of Israel, saith the Lord the God of hosts; and they shall afflict you from the entering in of Hemath unto the river of the wilderness." In the Hebrew language this phrase indicated that the process was already in motion. The wheels of God's justice were rolling. Assyria was flexing its muscles. The word "afflict" means to crush, to squeeze. Israel would be cruelly crushed beneath Assyria.

Would to God that modern America could learn from the plight of Israel. It's not too late. But God's chariot is in motion. Only in him can our unrighteousness be changed into righteousness. There are commitments we need to make. Consider his plan and purpose for your life. No genuine revival ensued from the preaching of Amos, but will we heed God's warning signs? I pray we will!

15
Trying God's Patience
(Amos 7:1-9)

In the seventh chapter we are immediately confronted with three different visions. Each is introduced by the statement, "Thus hath the Lord God shewed unto me . . . . " (vv. 1,4,7). Verses 1 and 2 refer to God's forming grasshoppers in the beginning of the shooting up of the latter growth; and lo, it was the latter growth after the king's mowings. And it came to pass, that when they had made an end of eating the grass of the land, then I said, O Lord God, forgive, I beseech thee: by whom shall Jacob arise? for he is small."

Here is a picture of a grasshopper or locust plague, and the plague arrived after the king had received his share. The custom was for the government to levy a tax on a farmer's crops or livestock, thus funding the government. Sound familiar? After the king received his share, the people lived off of the rest. Even after the king collected his share, though, the locusts descended and ate up the remainder. The people had nothing left with which to sustain life.

In verses 4 and 5 there is reference to "the Lord God called to contend by fire, and it devoured the great deep, and did eat up a part." You can imagine how devastating the fire was because it decimated the water supply—perhaps a drought is also indicated. The land was barren and parched when the fire swept across the land. The vegetation was destroyed, along with the water supply. Here the Lord paints a tragic picture of desolation, drought, famine, and thirst.

Read verse 7. "The Lord stood upon a wall made by a plumbline, with a plumbline in his hand." This was a symbol referring to God's measuring Israel according to straightness. It is interesting to note that after the grasshoppers and the fire, Amos prayed and God did not destroy the people. Here he did not pray. He was unable to pray and judgment would fall.

There are several truths in this passage. First, *God is in all the experiences of life.* There is the repeated phrase, "the Lord God shewed unto me." One translation has it: "The Lord God caused me to see." In the original language it meant that the Lord gave intimate knowledge to someone. God was declaring, even through disappointments and tragedies, "I am amid every experience." God would teach us to look beyond tragedy and behold his hand. In everything God's plan is being worked out. Nothing can happen to us without God being there. For the Christian every experience of God is graciously and lovingly couched in the presence and purpose of God. I think of a gospel song about the fact that God didn't bring us this far to let us down. He didn't teach us to swim to let us drown. God is not going to abandon us amid our situation. God is in every experience.

Second, *we are incapable of facing these experiences* alone. Mankind is helpless and hopeless. How can any honest human being shake his fist in the face of God and, with clenched teeth, mutter, "I don't need you, God"? They were powerless to stop the locusts. In spite of pesticides and modern technology, plagues are still common in Third World countries. How could they stop a vast conflagration? The fact is, even now we are not able to cope with what are still called "acts of God"— avalanches, hurricanes, tornados, tidal waves, earthquakes, mudslides, ravaging forest fires. With God, however, nothing can defeat us. Without God even physical life is impossible. Unless God is there, every moment of existence becomes insurmountable. He alone can give deep-down strength and victory. If you can't handle life without God, it's going to be even worse in judgment. Like the old hymn goes, "I must tell Jesus all of my trials, I cannot bear these burdens alone." We cannot make it alone.

The third comforting thought is: *God does respond to mankind's prayer.* Glance at verses 3 and 6. "The Lord repented. . . ." What does that mean? I do not think it implies that God had done wrong or that God had changed his mind. But it is a reminder that the will of God is not a harsh and unfeeling fate, but God has a loving concern for a frail and needy people. Our prayers miraculously release God to be loving and redemptive toward us. God answers prayer. God in his sovereignty and his purpose has designed that his will on this earth shall be wrought by prayer. I do not understand it. I cannot explain it. But prayer does it. I joyfully accept God's workings. With our two-by-four minds we cannot possibly begin to understand the height and depth and length and breadth of God.

Let me give you an example. Peter wrote that God is "not willing that any should perish, but that all should come to repentance" (2 Pet. 3:9). How is a person saved? By prayer, evidenced by repentance and faith. It is a prayer of faith which allows a person to enter into the purposes of God. Yet, that is precisely what God wanted all the time. Prayer releases what God desires, wants, and wills. God responds to genuine prayer.

Prayer is the mightiest untapped resource in the universe. The prayers of a handful of believers could transform our generation. I believe the prayers of Christians could release God's power in Communist countries. Yet, we also need to remember that God's wrath is operative as the response of his holiness against sin. But God is perpetual in his determination to save and to keep a people for himself.

We can always find a reason not to pray, but the basic reason is: We don't believe in its power. Prayer is marvelous because it allows us to enter into partnership with the eternal purposes of

God. Many of us cannot teach, cannot assume positions of leadership—but all of us can pray. In prayer we are participating in the providential purposes of God Almighty!

There is a fourth thought: *God's patience does have a limit*. That is the essence of verses 7-9. The prophet saw God standing on a wall with a plumbline in his hand. The plumbline stands for the truth that God measures accurately. The people of Israel could not be crooked and get by with it. The plumbline more than likely represented the standards of God's covenant. Israel had entered into that relationship with the Lord God, but they had become crooked and perverse. Like an adulterous mate, they had broken their vows with God. He had remained true and unadulterated to them. Israel's spiritual whoredoms had tried God's longsuffering and patience. God will not be perpetually patient with rebellion and sin.

It is intriguing that God stood on a wall "made by a plumbline." That wall was right from the beginning because the plumbline had been used in calculations. The fact is: That wall had the materials in it, from the beginning, which could insure its final acceptability. That's also true with your relationship to God. When you are born again, God places all of the ingredients within you. You have within you the potential for acceptance or rejection as to the quality of your Christian life. God is first of all a redeemer, but he is also the lawgiver. His love produces redemption but also aims for obedience to his wishes. If we forsake and shun his grace, then we lose fellowship—not salvation—with him. And we love him only because of his love for us.

So the Lord would measure Israel by his divine standards— and they would be found crooked. Amos also foresaw a time when the sites of religious worship would be destroyed. "And the high places of Isaac shall be desolate, and the sanctuaries of Israel shall be laid waste; and I will rise against the house of Jeroboam with the sword" (v. 9). Jeroboam had become king with certain conditions. In 1 Kings 11:31-32 God promised Jeroboam the northern tribes of Israel, leaving one tribe "for my servant David's sake, and for Jerusalem's sake." Then in verse 38 God made this covenant with Jeroboam: "And it shall be, if thou wilt hearken unto all that I command thee, and wilt walk in my ways, and do that is right in my sight, to keep my statutes and my commandments, as David my servant did; that I will be with thee, and build thee a sure house, as I built for David, and will give Israel unto thee." Jeroboam violated the covenant, even to the extent of mixing idolatry with the worship of Jehovah. God did rise up against the house of Jeroboam. Hear 1 Kings 14:16: "And he [the Lord] shall give Israel up because of the sins of Jeroboam, who did sin, and who made Israel to sin." Jeroboam broke all of his commitments to the Lord. God's patience does have a limit.

Finally, *God uses us because he loves us.* Verse 8 indicates that God would "set a plumbline in the midst of my people Israel." Not Baal's people or Chemosh's people, but the *Lord's people.* Why did God use Israel? The only answer I know is found in Deuteronomy 7:7-8:

> *The Lord did not set his love upon you, nor choose you, because ye were more in number than any people; for ye were the fewest of all people: But because the Lord loved you, and because he would keep the oath which he had sworn unto your fathers, hath the Lord brought you out with a mighty hand, and redeemed you out of the house of bondmen, from the hand of Pharaoh king of Egypt.*

There was the assurance of God to his people, Israel. And it applies to "the sons of Abraham" in Christ, those of us who have received Jesus Christ as our Messiah. Why has God allowed you to hear his gospel? Why has he handed you advantages and opportunities which many have not had? Why did he plant a heart hunger within you? Because you were good? Because you were deserving? No. A thousand times no! Why did he choose you? Because he loves you—that's why.

John wrote, "We love him, because he first loved us" (1 John 4:19). It's not natural and normal for us to love God. Paul declared that we are "by nature the children of wrath." We deserve the punishment of God for our sins. By ourselves we are capable of loving no one but ourselves. But you and I are the objects of God's never-changing, eternal love. God pity you if his great, eternal love cannot cause you to respond. His love.

That's why sin is such a devastation and a tragedy—because ours is a disobedience and rebellion against God's love. We can justify rebelling against a rapist or a thief, someone who hates and despises us. But what kind of person strikes against love? That is why the world has never understood the love of the Lord Jesus. Jesus could have rained down the fire of retribution from heaven, but he remained on the cross of Calvary. Instead of cursing his enemies, Jesus, with heaven on his face and in his heart, called out, "Father, forgive them, for they know not what they do!" That's why Stephen the martyr cried out, "Lord, lay not this sin to their charge."

The world cannot fathom that kind of forgiving love. How anyone could reject the love of the Savior is beyond me. If you have left Christ out of your life, if you have rebelled against him, if you have resisted his Spirit, it has been a slap against his eternal love!

16
Religious Opposition to the Truth
(Amos 7:10-17)

This passage forms an interlude in Amos's prophetic message. Here we have an encounter between him and Amaziah, perhaps the chief priest at Bethel. This sort of encounter gives us insight into the courage of Amos as he stood against the wicked leaders of Israel.

Even though this encounter breaks into the message, it is in line with the burdensome preaching Amos had been doing.

In verses 10 and 11 let's look at the accusations leveled against Amos: "Then Amaziah the priest of Bethel sent to Jeroboam king of Israel, saying, Amos hath conspired against thee in the midst of the house of Israel: the land is not able to bear all his words. For thus Amos saith, Jeroboam shall die by the sword, and Israel shall surely be led away captive out of their own land."

These two verses contain the *accusations* of Amaziah against Amos. Amaziah sent a message to King Jeroboam and made accusations, virtually accusing Amos of treason against the king and the government. But he tried to put words into Amos's mouth. From time immemorial this sort of device has been used by Satan's people in an attempt to ruin God's servants. People bent on evil try to misrepresent and twist the words of preachers. Amos had never conspired against Jeroboam. He had done nothing deserving this accusation. Such is often the case when a man of God follows the leading of the Lord in preaching the divine Word. Amaziah claimed that Amos was trying to stir up an

141

insurrection, a revolution against the king. He also charged that the people couldn't bear Amos's message. But that's often the case when a message is filled with condemnation and judgment. Yet, Amaziah was expressing his opinion and maybe speaking more for himself than anyone else.

There is no question that the people were disturbed about the strange prophet from Judah who delivered a fierce, uncompromising message.

But the Israelites were also not unmindful of their religious obligations. It was distasteful for them to realize that their religion was an affront and offense toward God. Amos had visited their shrines firsthand and had seen the hypocrisy and sham involved in their worship. He had thundered the truth that God was not pleased with their vain rituals and forms.

That was a bitter pill for them to swallow. Like us today they always thought of "those other people" as the "bad guys." So, Amaziah made the accusation that the people were not able to put up with all Amos's words. He also accused Amos of threatening the king's life. "Jeroboam shall die by the sword" Amos was quoted as preaching, but he had never done that directly. Yes, he had declared that judgment and captivity were coming, that the nation would fall, and that the kingdom of Jeroboam would crumble. But that is different from threatening the king with death and leading a revolution. Amos called for revolution within the hearts of the people, not with the implements of violence. "Israel shall surely be led away out of their own land" was the only accurate fact Amaziah had reported. In fact, Amos repeated that in verse 17: "Israel shall surely go into captivity forth of his land."

What Amaziah did was pick up a portion of Amos's message, magnify it, misrepresent it, and misapply it—as a classic example of taking things out of context and twisting them. In the accusation, however, there is a truth which affects any individual who lives for God. We can expect opposition. We can expect to be accused, to face trials, and to be tested. Peter counseled the Christians, "Beloved, think it not strange concerning the fiery trial which is to try you, as though some strange thing happened unto you" (1 Pet. 4:12). Don't be surprised when you're tested. He also taught us that "they who live godly in Christ Jesus shall also suffer persecution" (2 Tim. 3:12).

Expect Satan to rear his ugly head anytime you stand solidly upon God's Word and commit yourself to Christ. When you allow Jesus Christ to become Lord in your life, you not only receive a new Lord—you get a new enemy. Satan will make sure you are opposed and that you are tested. We have the mistaken notion that if we are in the center of God's will everything will go great, and there will be a smooth road ahead. I'm not sure God ever designed it like that. Sometimes you'll have a bumpy road, but Jesus will always be there to help absorb the shocks.

Amos was experiencing his lumps. His situation reminded me of Jesus' words, "For which of you intending to build a tower, sitteth not down first, and counteth the cost, whether he have sufficient to finish it? . . . Or what king, going to make war against another king, sitteth not down first, and consulteth whether he be able with ten thousand to meet him that cometh against him with twenty thousand? . . . So likewise, whosoever he be of you that forsaketh not all that he hath, he cannot be my disciple" (Luke 14:28,31,33). Count the cost. Amos had. We must have a commitment which is unafraid of the pressure and opposition that arise.

Now turn your thoughts to verses 12 and 13 which cover *the affront* to Amos. "Also Amaziah said unto Amos, O thou seer, go, flee thee away into the land of Judah, and there eat bread, and prophesy there. But prophesy not any more at Bethel: for it is the king's chapel, and it is the king's court." The affront was exactly that—straight and blatantly to the point. "Get lost. Get out of town. We don't want you here." Many preachers have heard those very words. First of all, the affront was sarcastic.

The word *seer* was originally a positive term to describe the prophets. The word spoke of a man's call from God and his divine insight to receive the message of the Lord and then share it with others. Yet, there was evidence that the word had evolved into "dreamer" or "stargazer." Amaziah was probably referring to Amos as a vain dreamer or even an astrologer.

"Flee away into the land of Judah." In the Hebrew the phrase carried the connotation of "fleeing for your own good." Amaziah thought that Amos was just "doing his own thing." He was not aware that Amos was a man driven by God. Amaziah appealed to making a living. Surely Judah was where Amos belonged— among the Jews where he could "make it" in familiar surroundings and where the people could understand him better. Regionalism in our own nation has died with difficulty. We still think of "Yankees" and "Rebels" and Easterners and Westerners and so forth. The country was divided between Israel and Judah. Amaziah was almost saying, "What do you mean, Rebel, coming up here trying to tell us Yankees how to live? Go back home and preach against Israel, and they'll yell *Amen*. You'll receive a warm reception." To Amaziah there was every reason for Amos to leave. The message. The locale. The circumstances. The possible repercussions. The mixed response of the populace. The affront was, in whatever words, "Get outta here and don't come back!"

There was Amos's *answer* in 14 and 15. "Then answered Amos and said to Amaziah, I was no prophet, neither was I a prophet's son; but I was an herdman, and a gatherer of sycamore fruit; And the Lord took me as I followed the flock, and the Lord said unto me, Go prophesy unto my people Israel." "The Lord took me" is fraught with meaning. Prophesying was not Amos's idea. It seems he was content with his farming occupation. He tended the flocks and gathered the fruit, minding his own business. But Amos didn't have the say-so. God *took* him. If you please, God conscripted Amos into divine service. Amaziah faced a man who was doing what he *had* to do. He was not preaching because he wanted to—but because God commanded him. Amos was not trained as a prophet or a priest. We would call him a layman, a lay preacher. Yet God prepared him. God chose and selected him. When God does that, you'd better not fight. Amos was practicing what he had preached.

In Amos 3:8 the prophet had testified, "The lion hath roared, who will not fear? the Lord God hath spoken, who can but prophesy?" Amos answered, "I can't help it. I have no choice. I didn't vote to come here. I didn't especially want to deliver this message. God put it in my heart and commanded me to proclaim his word." Every genuine preacher and prophet of God has a divinely given authority.

Throughout the Old Testament we read about the compulsions of the prophets. Let's face it—prophets were not popular people. I doubt if they would have made it into "Who's Who." They laid heavy proclamations on the people. Number one, they repeatedly warned of God's condemnation of their wickedness and of God's impending judgment. Think about Jeremiah, "the weeping prophet." Is it a wonder he wept over the sins of Judah? Tradition has it that his own people carried him into Egypt. There they became so infuriated with him that they laid him between two pieces of wood and cut him in two with a saw. He was "sawn asunder" for his prophesy.

God had called him: "Before I formed thee in the belly, I knew thee; and before thou camest forth out of the womb I sanctified thee, and I ordained thee a prophet unto the nations" (Jer. 1:5). God sanctified and ordained Jeremiah long before he was conceived in his mother's womb. Then Jeremiah protested, "Ah, Lord God! behold, I cannot speak: for I am a child" (v. 6). It is thought by many that Jeremiah actually was a child when God called him. Whether or not he was makes no difference. God provided the empowerment: "Say not, I am a child; for thou shalt go to all that I shall send thee, and whatsoever I command thee thou shalt speak" (v. 7). As a symbol of God's enabling, "The Lord put forth his hand, and touched my mouth. And the Lord said unto me, Behold, I have put my words in thy mouth" (v. 9).

Over and over again Jeremiah wrote, "Thus saith the Lord," "The word of the Lord came to me, saying . . . , " and similar expressions. In Jeremiah 20:9 the prophet's frustration overflowed after preaching to a wicked, gainsaying people: "Then I said, I will not make mention of him, nor speak any more in his name. But his word was in mine heart as a burning fire shut up in my bones, and I was weary with forbearing, and I could not stay." In other words, delivering the frightful message of judgment was almost more than the prophet himself could endure. It elicited hatred and vituperation from the people— and that will happen whenever the man of God is being a prophet.

Jeremiah, at that point, had virtually promised himself, "I'm not going to face them anymore. I'm not going to mention God's name. But the word of God is burning within me and I had to let it out. I can't keep quiet." Why? Because he was speaking God's words.

There is no better definition of inspiration than in Jeremiah 1:9: "I have put my words in thy mouth." That is how we received the Scriptures. Was it God's words or Jeremiah's words? God's or Amos's? It was the prophet's words, but God directed him what to speak and write. When Amos spoke, God was speaking. When Jeremiah spoke, God was speaking. The prophets had received a commission to be God's mouthpieces, God's spokesmen.

Amos *had* to deliver the message. He had no alternatives. Our lack of this compulsion is one of the deadly tragedies of American Christianity. I am convinced that the greatest work of God today is not in this nation. Our brand of Christianity is one of convenience. Let it rain. We'll do what we'd never do in relation to our jobs (jobs are too scarce). But we'll let rain keep us from church. Seldom do we have concern for the souls of our friends, neighbors, and relatives. We often attend church to have our souls fed and we become spiritually bloated. Doesn't it make us feel comfortable to come with our cups and expect the water of life, and then not share a drop of it with a gospel-thirsty world?

And everytime the preacher or the Sunday School director or a staff member talks with us about what we ought to do, we protest: "Hey, wait a minute, preacher. You're dealing with volunteers. The staff ought to go out and do that. After all you're being too hard on us." That's not true. None of us are volunteers. You are not your own—you are bought with the price of the precious blood of the Lord Jesus Christ. It is not for you to determine whether it is convenient for you to serve God. If you're truly born again, you have no choice. If you have received Christ, you've already chosen. What's the big deal? You and I are to give ourselves unstintingly, unquestionably, and unreservedly to do God's will in our lives. We are to be what God wants us to be.

The New Testament church, with all its inexperience and faults, had a compulsion, an obsession. The members were viciously persecuted so they were scattered abroad and dispersed all over the known world—which made it all the better for them to proclaim the name of Jesus. "They that were scattered abroad went everywhere preaching the word" (Acts 8:4). The pastors, by and large, stayed in Jerusalem. The laity shook the known world. They *had* to do it. The early church, some contended, moved in power because of the sheer excitement and adventure of following Jesus. There was a life-and-death risk involved. It was dangerous to be a Christian. Jesus had told his early followers, "Go your ways: behold, I send you forth as lambs among wolves" (Luke 10:3).

No, we are not volunteers for God. We have been drafted into his army. We exist for one reason—to give glory to God. And our alibis are multitudinous. I've heard them all. "I don't have time." "I must have more time for relaxation." "I don't have the resources." "I don't have time with my family." Also, when we selfishly try to do what only God can do, we destroy what we are trying to protect. We have built an army in which only the general fight, and we're losing the battle. Enter the fray even if it means being a buck private or a plebe. Listen, you will destroy your life, your home, your vocation, everything about you if you selfishly seek to reserve yourself for your own self-interest and self-gratification. God has called us, and we'd best speak.

Camp now on verse 16: "Now therefore hear thou the word of the Lord: Thou sayest, Prophesy not against Israel, and drop not thy word against the house of Isaac. Therefore thus saith the Lord; . . . " Amos made an *affirmation* of God's truthfulness. Judgment was passed upon Amaziah, his wife, his children, his property. Amos's prophecy was coming home to none other than his accuser. Amaziah heard the word of the Lord but fought it, rebelled against it—and flagrantly opposed God's messenger.

It's always like that. The sinner gets it in the neck. He can never rebel against God without doing harm to himself. There is a moral law written into the character and nature of God himself—God's holiness cries out in wrath and mankind's disobedience. Amaziah was simply reaping the result of disregarding the word of the Lord. There was the affirmation: "Thus saith the Lord."

Earlier in chapter 7 Amos had spoken about the plumbline. "Thus he shewed me: and behold, the Lord stood upon a wall made by a plumbline, with a plumbline in his hand. And the Lord said unto me, Amos, what seest thou? And I said, A plumbline. Then said the Lord, Behold, I will set a plumbline in the midst of my people Israel: and I will not again pass by them any more" (7:7-8). A plumbline since its invention has aided us in checking the straightness of an object—a brick wall, a building, a fence. Here it stood for God's standards. God places his plumbline in the lives of individuals and nations. And God gauged Amaziah by heavenly standards, and Amaziah didn't measure up. Amaziah was not what he claimed to be. He was, in the words of Daniel's prophecy, "weighed in the balances and found wanting." Wait a minute. How do you measure up? Straight or crooked? How do you stack up alongside the clear commands of God's Word? Instead of comparing our lives to others, we ought to check ourselves compared to the Word of God. God never asked us to look at others for our personal measurements. He asked us to look up. Romans 3:23 doesn't say, "For all have sinned and come short of the glory of the average"—but "all have sinned and come short of the glory of God."

Now a personal confession. We claim to believe the Word but don't practice it. Several years ago in Dallas I rescued a family of our neighbors from their burning house at 1 o'clock in the morning. According to the fire chief, I saved their lives—a mother and her three children. They lived there for over a year and a half, and I never did tell them about Jesus. I was more concerned about their physical lives than their spiritual. I indict myself. Why did I keep quiet? Why do you do the same? If we had anything to share, we'd share it. We can't share what we don't possess. We don't share what's unfavorable to us. We don't share anything we have qualms about. What does that say about our sharing of Jesus Christ?

There needs to be an affirmation about the Word of God. One time on our sign in front of the church there was this slogan: "There are two parts of the gospel, Believing it and behaving it."

We must understand that we are to measure ourselves by the Word. Israel was in a bad shape, but I wonder how much better off we are today. We are kin to the Israelites.

We must be possessed by a compulsion to proclaim the word of the Lord, the kind of constraint which captured Amos.

17
A Basket of Summer Fruit
(Amos 8:1-3)

Thus hath the Lord God shewed unto me: and behold a basket of summer fruit. And he said, Amos, What seest thou? And I said, a basket of summer fruit. Then said the Lord unto me. The end is come upon my people Israel. I will not again pass by them any more. And the songs of the temple shall be the howling in that day, saith the Lord God: There shall be many dead bodies in every place; they shall cast them forth with silence.

The setting was in the fall of the year. We are aware of the warnings, the signs, and messages of impending judgment Amos had delivered to the nation. Throughout the Book of Amos he had cried, "repent or God is going to bring judgment." He continued to warn the people of the coming judgment of God, but always he gave an appeal to repentance, an invitation to forgiveness and to a response by the people. Amos taught that judgment was coming but God was gracious.

Up until this point there had been the hope of forgiveness, redemption, and restoration on the part of the people. Now we have reached a point in this passage beyond which God could not go in his mercy and grace. He picked a setting of a fall festival, the Feast of Booths, which we find described in Deuteronomy 16. It was a time in the fall of the year; I suppose it would be similar to our Thanksgiving. It was a period when the people gathered all the blessings of God, the bounty of the harvest, and the provisions God had led them to have. They would then bring token offerings or sacrifices out of the blessings of God. They would come to the place of sacrifice and offer to God thanksgiving, and it would be a season of blessing and praising God.

It was a time for them to be reminded that in a unique sense, they belonged to God. They were God's people. They were in a covenant relationship with him. They walked in fellowship with God and in harmony with his purposes. That is the setting of this passage, and it is as though God and Amos walked in and watched the people bringing their sacrifices and offerings. Theirs was a basket of fruit. The harvest time was past. It was after summer, they gave summer fruit, which means it was almost past due; it would be the last crop of fruit they would have. In that situation God cast a bitter word. God said, "It is fruit but it is ripe fruit. It is fruit but it has matured. It is fruit from the end harvest of the crop. What you are really ripe for is judgment!"

There is a play on words here that does not express itself well in English. There are two words here that are very much alike. Summer fruit is a particular word in the Hebrew, and the word "the end" sounds a lot like it in Hebrew. God was saying, "You have brought summer fruit, but I say they really have come *as* summer fruit." The people brought that which represented the end of the season, but in reality they themselves had come to the end of the season. They had come to the end of God's patience. They themselves have reached the place beyond which God could not go. There was a dreadful harvest time ahead. The end of the season of repentance had come. Their religion had utterly failed to alert them to God and to his judgment upon their lives.

There is a New Testament counterpart to this truth. In Hebrews 6:4-6 there is a description of a conversion experience, and the writer of Hebrews wrote that "it is impossible" for those at a certain point to be renewed "again unto repentance." I believe that means God's own children can reach the place that they fall under the judgment of God physically, socially, nationally, and personally, and are unable again to repent. They go beyond God's grace in that sense. They do not lose their salvation, but God's judgment falls upon them as a people. This is what we behold here in Israel. The people had been recipients of God's grace; they had been blessed abundantly by God and chosen of God. They had heard the messages of God, but they had twisted and perverted justice and faith. Their worship had become little more than form and ritual. They had no heart, no compassion, no reaching out for God or for the world about them. And God said, "You don't come with summer fruit. You *are* summer fruit. You have come to the end of the season when you can repent. Judgment must come."

Now notice two things in this passage (and the fruit and its application are relevant for us today). First, there was *the ripening of human conduct*. In verse 2, Amos is asked, "What do you see," and he answered, "A basket of summer fruit." God said, "The end is come upon my people of Israel; I will not again pass by them any more." Amos drew upon nature. He reminded the people that nature is governed by cycles. You have spring, summer, autumn, winter. You have planting, cultivating, and harvest. Nature has an endless cycle of maturation, and yet each season is unique in its own. No crop really carries over to another time. There are planting, cultivation, and harvest. That forms a unit of thought for Amos. There is a beginning, a maturing, and a consummation.

That is the truth of nature. God is saying to the people and to us that this is a symbol for the ripening of human conduct. Our own lives, our characters, our conduct, our relationships with God will either mature or deteriorate. They will move toward full development for good or for evil. We do not ever stay the same. We are constantly maturing, so we must understand the ripening of human conduct. I hear people talking about "holding my own. I'm not doing very well. I'm just holding my own." No, you're not, you don't hold your own. If you're not moving forward for God, you are moving away from God. If you are not maturing in your commitment to Christ, you are moving away in rebellion against Christ. If you are not moving positively toward the goal of God for your life, then you are moving away. Growth is like that. There is no treadmill of the spirit.

We've all grown since we were born. I don't ever remember a time when I sat down and watched myself grow. As a child about the only way I would realize I had grown was when I put on a pair of pants I had not worn in a couple of months. I had the experience one summer that some of you did. I grew six inches one summer! I remember when fall came and I had to wear some school clothes that I had in the spring, they looked like knickers! They suddenly seemed shorter. I had grown. I had changed. I wasn't aware of it but I had changed. That is a truth which is as practical to our lives physically and spiritually as it can possibly be. There comes a ripening of human conduct. We are either becoming more like Christ or less like him. You never drift anywhere worth going. There has to be a diligence, a discipline toward the kind of growth God wants us to have.

The Bible speaks often about this kind of digression. When God created the world, he gave his perfect fellowship to Adam and Eve. You well know the story of Adam and Eve's sin, and the subsequent way sin began to work in the hearts of mankind. Those back in those days who walked in close harmony with God, knew the sound of his voice, and knew the sense of his presence, had fellowship with him. In spite of all they had, because of a lack of obedience and discipline, they moved away from God. Then we come to Genesis 6:5-7. God saw the heart of mankind was nothing but "evil continually," and God felt sorry that he had made man. Judgment came because there was a downward digression from God. That's how it happens.

A person who does not give himself to seek God, will turn away from God. One who does not give himself in obedience to God will find himself in opposition to God. One who does not give himself in repentance to God, will find himself condemned by God. It is a digression that is automatic. You do not have to sow weeds in a garden. You merely leave it alone; the weeds will grow naturally. The garden does not stay the same. It will either progress toward harvest or it will move toward uselessness. Our lives are like that. There is a ripening of human conduct. It is tragic in the spiritual sense because there are many folks who haven't grown spiritually in years. You can tell it. If they ever give a testimony, it's always what happened ten years ago, twenty years ago. They talk about some dim day in the past or about how spiritual they want to be. They have no interest in witnessing for Christ or being a part of praying for others or ministering in a community. For them it is always something else out there.

They move away from God because they have not moved toward him. That's our responsibility and our opportunity. Whatever being made "in the image of God" means, it implies that we can direct our hearts toward God if we choose to do so. That is what God expects of us as he draws us to himself. He wants our willingness, our obedience to him.

Yet, there is a digression of human conduct which usually expresses itself in contempt of God's message. It was true in Amos 2 how the people had compromised the Nazarites who had taken a vow never to drink wine. Yet many people gave the Nazarites wine to drink. Likewise they commanded the prophets, saying, "Don't prophesy." In chapter 7 Amaziah said to Amos, "Don't prophesy here anymore. Don't preach here anymore. We don't want to hear what you have to say. Go somewhere else." Our downward movement away from God generally expresses itself in contempt for God's message and messenger. "Don't bother me with the Scriptures. Don't trouble me with God's word. I have a right." Rebellious people find themselves in disharmony with the purposes of God. They don't want to hear God's message. They'll find every reason not to.

Maybe we don't like the preacher. Maybe we don't like the teacher. Maybe we don't like the church. Maybe we don't like this or that. Somehow we will find our alibi, but the truth is, whenever we are not moving towards God, we are negatively moving away from him. If we are not closer to God today than we ever have been, if Jesus is not more precious to us than he ever has been, then we are moving away from God. You remember the time when you were so in love with Jesus that you couldn't sing the hymns because you were so choked up? Remember the time you could merely think about God's blessings and tears would come to your eyes? Love would well in your heart. What happened to you?

Oh, you answer, "You don't know the trouble I'm in right now. You don't know the heartache, the pressures I've had to face in my family and my business. You don't know the conflict and the difficulty that have arisen."

Those are all opportunities for God to reveal himself to you. The greatest knowledge we ever have of God is the understanding of God that involves him in the difficulties of life and gives victory over those difficulties. Every difficulty, every opposition, every pressure is an opportunity for God to reveal himself in our lives afresh and anew. Trouble is an opportunity for God to show us he is able, for God to reveal his perfect will to us. Every disappointment, every discouragement, every point of pressure becomes an opportunity for God to do a significant work in our lives. Don't let those things drive you away from God. Let them drive you to him. There is a ripening of human conduct.

Secondly, there is a reaping of human conduct. We get what we sow. Don't blame anybody else with your problems. The devil didn't make you do it. You reap what you sow. Paul nailed down in Galatians 6:7. "Be not deceived, God is not mocked. Whatsoever a man soweth, that shall he also reap. He that soweth to his flesh, shall of his flesh reap corruption. He that soweth to the Spirit shall of the Spirit reap life everlasting." I

Numbers 32:23 Joshua said essentially the same. "You can do what you wish if that's your desire, if that's your commitment, but you'll be sinning if you do, and you can be sure that your sin will find you out." There is always a reaping of human conduct.

In verse 3 there is a tragic description of what the end will be. He writes about the joyful song and the festivals ending in sad, somber wailings. He writes about the death and burial of many people, a day of great judgment and despair, and this despair will displace the easy confidence of the people. "That day" refers back to "the day of the Lord" in Amos 5:18-20, when Amos reminded the people that they were talking about wanting the Lord to come. But Amos indicated, "When he comes, it is going to be more dark than it is light. There is going to be a time of bitterness and weeping." Amos said, "Woe to you that desire the day of the Lord. What is it to you? The day of the Lord is darkness and not light. As a man did flee from a lion and a bear met him, or went into the house, leaned on the wall, and a serpent bit him, shall not the day of the Lord be darkness and not light, even very dark and not brightness in it?" Amos is simply reminding us we need to be aware that God's judgment is severe.

We talk about revival. We don't want genuine revival. We can talk about it piously and sing about it if you want to, but we don't really want revival, because if revival came, it would absolutely consume everything contrary to the Holy Spirit, and that would about devastate most of us! It's not going to be a happy, bright day. Don't think of revival as some theoretical emotional-type, hallelujah time—that's not revival. Revival is when God's Spirit moves in hearts, and the day of the Lord—the day of God's presence—is stirring in our midst. First, God has to deal with sin, our rebellion, and lethargy—and then he can bless. First there had to be a death before there could be a resurrection. That's true in our relationship with the Lord. There is a reaping of human conduct.

If God is to deal with us, he will have to do it brutally at some point. There are things in our lives which God's Spirit and presence cannot at all tolerate. I want you to notice two or three facts about it. First, I want you to notice its *scope*. It includes everyone of us. No one is exempt from it.

Paul wrote:

> *None of us liveth unto himself, and no man dieth unto himself. For whether we live, we live unto the Lord; and whether we die, we die unto the Lord; whether we live therefore, or die, we are the Lord's. For to this end Christ both died, and rose, and revived, that he might be the Lord both of the dead and living. . . . For it is written, every knee shall bow to me, and every tongue shall confess to God. So then every one of us shall give account of himself to God (Rom. 14:7-9, 11-12).*

It includes all of us. The scope of the reaping does not escape one of us. All of us are accountable and responsible. We must stand and face God in this matter. That's the scope. But it includes everything we do. Look in Luke 12:2-3. "There is nothing covered that shall not be revealed; neither hid, that shall not be known. Therefore, whatsoever ye have spoken in darkness shall be heard in the light; and that which ye have spoken in the ear in closets shall be proclaimed upon the housetops." In Matthew 12:36-37, Jesus said, "But this I say unto you, That every idle word that men shall speak, they shall give account thereof in the day of judgment, For by thy words thou shalt be justified, and by thy words thou shalt be condemned."

Jesus included "Every idle word." If every idle word is something we are accountable to God for, then it is extremely important what we do in our casual relationships, isn't it? If it's important enough for God to judge it, then it can't be inconsequential. Oh, you say, "I didn't mean that. I was just joking." Really? Jesus stressed *every idle word*. You're going to be responsible for all of them. No word is casual, off the cuff, off

the record. Every idle word! The world could be immensely
sweetened and the cause of Christ enhanced greatly if we
Christians would guard our words. The reaping of our human
conduct will be very exacting. It reaches into everything we are,
everything we say, everything we do.

In the Book of Ecclesiastes, writing to young people, "The
Preacher" says, "Rejoice, O young man, in thy youth; and let
thy heart cheer thee in the days of thy youth, and walk in the
ways of thine heart, and in the sight of thine eyes: but know
thou, that for all these things God will bring you into judgment"
(11:9). In the last verse of Ecclesiastes, it says "For God shall
bring every work into judgment, with every secret thing,
whether it be good or whether it be evil" (12:14).

Christianity is the way we are. It is the way of thinking, the
way of speaking, the way of acting, the way of living, the way of
responding, reacting, and relating. It involves everything we are,
and we shall reap the consequences of our conduct in every one
of these areas.

Now, I want you to notice that we reap accurately; although
down here we may misunderstand and misjudge, God never
does. The Bible indicates that God is keeping a book, and Jesus
spoke of every idle word. God is writing it all down. When we
reap the consequences of our conduct, you can be sure it will be
accurate. Someone may protest, "Well, God, I'm not as bad as it
seems." Yet God answers, "It's in the book. Here is the book,
and here's what it says."

"But Lord, I loved souls more than you think I did." How
many times have you really prayed for the lost? How many times
have you concerned yourself for those who didn't know Christ?
It's in the book. Here it is. "But Lord, I believed in prayer. I trusted
you more than some people." *It's in the book, and here it is.* No
mistaking, it is absolutely accurate. God knows, God understands, and God records it, and we are going to reap what we
have sown. Many of the adversities that come to us, even in this

life, are the result of reaping what we have sown. It is an accurate recording of what we are.

Now, Israel could raise many objections. "Lord, look, we have all these worship services, all these shrines, these choirs, rabbis up there preaching—everything is going great. We have given huge sums of money to missions. Lord, look at us." They could have put up many arguments because religion flourished in Israel. Shrines grew up everywhere, and the people who crowded to the shrines were meticulously faithful. God said, "You are a basket of summer fruit. I'll not pass again by Israel." The season had ended.

The writer of Hebrews (Heb. 4:13), for instance, talked about the responsibility which is ours before God: "Neither is there any creature that is not manifest in his sight." The word *manifest* means known fully, completely. All things are naked and unclothed under the eyes of him with whom we have to do. Nothing is hidden from God. We must understand that our accuser is God himself, the One to whom we are responsible. He is God.

In 1 Corinthians 4:1-5, the Apostle Paul wrote:

> Let a man so account of us, as the ministers of Christ, and stewards of the mysteries of God, Moreover it is required in stewards, that a man be found faithful. But with me it is a very small thing that I should be judged of you, or of man's judgment: yea, I judge not mine own self. For I know nothing by myself: . . . he that judgeth me is the Lord.

In 2 Timothy 4:1, Paul, writing to young Timothy, said, "I charge you therefore before God, and the Lord Jesus Christ, who shall judge the quick and the dead at his appearing and in his kingdom." In verse 8 of the same chapter Paul speaks of "the crown of righteousness, which the Lord, the righteous judge, shall give me at that day." Rev. 20:11 tells about God who sits upon the throne and judges.

My point is: We are not being judged on the basis of human opinion or what people think we are. We will not be judged by what people think we did and why we did it, but we will be judged according to what God knows to be true. He is the Arbitrator and the Judge. He is the One who will oversee the reaping and the harvest. We are going to have a harvest and God is going to oversee it.

When souls are saved and there is a harvest of people committing their lives to Jesus Christ, God did it. God did it! The harvest is his. When we confront evil and God moves in our lives, and when marvelous victory is experienced, God did it! David declared, "The battle is the Lord's." It's his. He did it! When you reap the harvest of rebellion, God did that, too. Do not think that God is going to give a harvest of blessing without giving a harvest of bitterness, if our lives are in rebellion against him. You can be sure that the One who was behind the statement, "All things work together for good to them that love God, to them who are the called according to his purpose," will bring what is best for you out of every experience. The same God will see to it that you reap what you sow if you rebel against him.

For Israel the season had ended. "A basket of summer fruit" signified that there was no time for repentance. But for us there is yet time for commitment. For us there is an invitation to his grace. For us there is an opportunity to accept and taste his mercy. We can repent. God has given us an opportunity—he has placed his Word in our hearts and we can repent. The most pressing need in my life and our lives together as a church and a nation is for an honest reaching out to God in repentance, letting him touch our lives and do what he pleases in us.

Unless that happens, the most devastating days in our history lie ahead of us. I do not believe there is any hope apart from a supernatural movement of God. God has chosen to work through human instrumentality. Don't expect God to send a lightning bolt down from heaven to activate a missile headed for this land. God is going to work the supernatural through the lives of natural people, and the only hope in this earth is for God to have liberty with which to perform his miraculous power, to move supernaturally through our lives. We have the unprecedented opportunity to be the vehicles through which God could usher in a mighty moving of his Spirit throughout this land. We also have within our hearts the opportunity to answer *no* to him and to continue in our lethargy and unconcern, playing games, toying with fate, mocking God with our inconsistency.

The choice is ours, but believe me: Before many months pass, if that does not happen, God is going to reveal America as a basket of summer fruit. The season is almost over—the choice is ours!

18
Imminent Judgment
(Amos 8:4-14)

This passage falls into three basic divisions which are clearly defined, and specifically applied to our hearts. First of all in verses 4-7, notice the *covetousness* of the people. We have sort of a reminder of what Amos has hit periodically throughout the book.

Those in control of the society have been oppressing the poor, taking advantage of those less fortunate than they. They lived for material things, the things of the world, for their own selfishness, their own egos. They had felt self-sufficient, arrogant in their rebellion and defiance against God. In the first verse Amos simply reminds us of the covetousness within man. He talks about how they "swallow up the needy, even to make the poor of the land to fail, Saying, When will the new moon be gone, that we may sell corn? and the sabbath, that we may set forth wheat, making the ephah small, and the shekel great, and falsifying the balances by deceit?" He lashed out against their mistreatment of the poor, and God declared, "Surely I will never forget this. I will never forget any of their works." The covetousness of mankind is incredible.

The people of Israel had come to the place where they loved things and possessions more than they loved God. They could hardly wait for the holy day to be over. They had a day away but they did not have a day off. Even while they were in the place of worship and going through the rituals of worship, it was obvious that their minds were in the marketplace. Their minds were back there doing business. They could not wait to increase their profits and to oppress the poor.

It is apparent that they did not have any genuine interest in worship of God; they loved possessions and profits. They loved greed more than they loved God. We have a prime example of this attitude in our own hearts. If you will study the etymology of the word *worship*, how the word came about, you will find that one of its parent words meant to "stop doing what you're doing." Worship means to stop what you are doing, pulling aside from the cares, pressures, despair, and discouragement of life. We are to draw aside and focus in on God. To worship really means that we come away from the things that crowd our minds and we zero in on God. We turn our attention to him.

But few people are able to do that, to give that kind of undivided attention; even while I preach sometimes I am distracted. If I blurted out some of my thoughts while I was preaching, you would be absolutely amazed. Many times while we are studying, praying, or even in the worship service, our minds are out there crowded with a thousand cares, the pressures, the undone job, the opportunity we may miss, the matter that is hanging over us, and we are unable to pull aside and worship God. Many people in Amos's day loved the things of the world more than they loved God, and if you find yourself unable to draw apart, so do you! If you find yourself unable to close the door, to shut the mind, to zero in on the awesomeness of approaching a holy and omnipotent God, then you too may have succumbed to the same kind of subtle covetousness to which the Israelites yielded. These people loved their greed.

More than that they loved their profit more than they loved honesty. Read the passage. They were going to sell wheat and make the ephah small and the shekel great. They were going to charge more than something was worth, and then they were going to give less than they charged their customers for. They were going to make a "pound" less, 12 ounces instead of 16, yet they were going to charge for 16 ounces. It was brazen dishonesty. It was a lack of responsibility.

They loved their work and what they possessed more than integrity. Where is integrity? Where is the person who will do a day's work for a day's pay? Where is the worker who will give you his word and do it? Where is the individual who will stand upon his commitment? Where is that person? There are few. We have in Southern Baptist churches alone more than 13,800,000 people who have declared, "We belong to Christ. He is our Savior, He is our Lord." And we can't find half of them! Where are they? They are not people of their word. They have no concern for personal integrity. Another 20 percent occasionally float in and out of the church, but as far as being a part of what God is doing in a community, sharing Christ, and touching the world for the Lord, they are not there. They love the world more than honesty and integrity.

I personally believe that the day is coming when it's going to cost us dearly to be Christians, and we're going to find out where true integrity is. A person who says "I am a Christian" won't be able to fake it. He's either going to be a Christian or not. I believe that testing time will be an abundant blessing to the church, for we have gone through a day of ease and lack of commitment—irresponsibility and lack of dedication are the norm. We have come to expect mediocrity of others and of ourselves. Those people of Israel loved material things, loved themselves, loved their greed more than their own integrity.

More than that they loved their profit more than mercy. They were trying to oppress the poor for silver and the needy for a pair of shoes. They were cheating the people, oppressing the poor. They were unmerciful people. Listen to me: It is impossible for us to obtain mercy if we are not giving mercy. It is inconceivable that a person would demand mercy for themselves and not give it to someone else. Remember the story that Jesus told in the parables? A certain man owed a great debt to his master, and the master forgave him. Then the forgiven man recalled that someone owed him a debt, and he sent that fellow to jail over it.

The master, hearing about that injustice, reinstated the debt and sent the unjust man to jail. The master punished him and condemned him because of his injustice and lack of mercy towards others.

One of the direst dangers of our day is the pernicious spirit of covetousness toward the things of this world and our selfishness as we demand things for ourselves without giving to other people. Why should you be forgiven if you are unforgiving? Why should you have mercy shown you if you don't show mercy to others? In fact Jesus declared in Matthew 6:14-15: "If ye forgive men their trespasses against you, your heavenly Father will forgive you. But if you forgive them not, neither will your Father forgive you your trespasses." He is saying that the only way to have forgiveness is through a repentant, open heart in faith to God. But one who would reach out in faith to God, yet condemn his brother and fail to show mercy and forgiveness to his brother, hasn't really reached God. Mercy and forgiveness are impossible for that person. These people loved their greed more than mercy. They wanted mercy for themselves but not for others. We must be wary of this subtle spirit of covetousness which puts other things before God, before integrity, before mercy and compassion that ought to characterize our lives.

The second idea I want you to notice is the *convulsions* around these people. Verses 8-10 form a trouble passage of Scripture. Two areas of tremendous shaking, tremendous convulsions are there. First, the earth, the land shall tremble for this. Then he speaks about floods, the sun going down at noon, and the earth being darkened at noonday. Amos deals with the devastation and the revolt of nature—and then convulsions within worship itself. Just as nature was in turmoil, worship was in chaos, for the passage covers feasts being turned into mourning and their songs into lamentations and sack cloth, and so on . . . the mourning of an only son. "The end thereof is a bitter day." What a tragic description. Now it treats two thoughts.

The revolt and turmoil of nature and the chaos of worship. I believe that the explanation of the uncertainties and tragedies that often afflict the world through natural laws is the result of sin. Romans 8 states that the whole creation groans, waiting for the redemption that Christ shall consummate when he comes. When he shall come, mankind shall be redeemed, but this earth shall also be redeemed. I cannot understand it all, but I do believe that the turmoil in nature is one result of the rebellion of man against God. Each natural occurrence and turmoil is an attempt by God to bring us back to him.

God states later in the passage, "I sent famine in the land. I sent drought in the land." These might be construed to be natural disasters, but God declared that he sent them to call his people to repentance. I fully believe the experiences of life are meant to drive us to God. You answer, "Well, you don't understand what I'm going through." Hear me. It is allowed by an omnipotent, sovereign God who desires to woo you to him.

Carol Ann and I recently went to HEB Hospital, where a dear man, around forty years old, was dying with cancer. He knew he was going to die, we talked about it. He said, "Preacher, you got a minute?" I certainly did. I sat down and he began to pour out his heart. He said, "You know I'm not going to come through one of these nights, and here's what I want." He began to share his faith and what he wanted for his funeral.

"I want Brother Don to sing 'The King Is Coming' and 'I Asked the Lord.' Preacher, the Lord moved in our hearts when we were courting. We knew we loved each other, but we didn't know if it was God's will, and a singer sang 'I Asked the Lord,' and God spoke to us through it, and I'd like to have that at my funeral.

"I want to ask a favor of you," he continued. "I want you and Don to come to Round Rock. I know it's a long way, but I want you to go with my family." We talked about the service, but we even laughed a little bit. It didn't seem out of place because he had Jesus. The inexplicable which no one can defy, no one can predict, no one can understand was happening. That experience had carried him to the throne of God. "I'm not apprehensive, I'm not frightened. I'm ready," he said. "Is it wrong for me to feel that way, Preacher? Seems like I should feel some other way." I said, "No, That's what our faith is all about." That tragedy later carried him to the Father.

He left an eleven-year-old son who won't understand, a young wife with many needs, a sister, a mom and dad. A crisis to them, a crucial time for them, and all of us are going through such sooner than we think. Maybe you have stood on the brink of death, or some of you have looked into the casket at the face of a loved one recently, or some of you have faced the disappointments and reversals of life. These are intended by a gracious God to draw you to him. You can let those experiences drive you away from him, and if so you turn toward despair and darkness where there is no answer, where there is not even a pinpoint of hope that ever shines into your darkened heart. Or you can let tragedies which baffle your mind and frighten your heart lead you to God. The choice is yours.

The people in Amos's day did not listen like that dear brother. They allowed the occurrences and turmoils of nature and life to drive them away from God. Their worship was in a shambles. When they should have been singing they were lamenting. When they ought to have been feasting, they were mourning. Sackcloth which represents despair and helplessness characterized their worship. God called it a bitter day (v. 10). Understand this: The judgments of God are not reserved for eternity alone. If this passage teaches us anything at all, it is that the judgments of God are seen in the ordinary events of life, and the hand of God will come upon our lives even in the mundane, humdrum things of life. There were convulsions all around them. Notice starting with verse 11 *the confusion* that was within them. "Behold, the days come, saith the Lord God, that I will send a famine in the land, not a famine of bread, nor a thirst for water, but of hearing the words of the Lord. And they shall wander from sea to sea, and from the north even to the east, and they shall run to and fro to seek the word of the Lord, and shall not find it. In that day shall the fair virgins and young men faint with thirst. They that swear by the sin of Samaria, and say, Thy God, O Dan, liveth; and, The manner of Beersheba liveth; even they shall fall, and never rise up again.

I want you to notice in this confusion some truths that are practical for our lives. God had withdrawn from them the blessings they despised. God spoke to them, they rejected it, God revealed his Word to them, and they would have none of it. God sent his prophets to them to prophesy, and they said, "Shut up." God had revealed his Word to them, but that which they despised he withdrew from them. Earlier the famine and the drought had been sent to drive them to God, but it had no results in their lives. Now God said, "I'm going to give you another famine. A famine of the Word. You will want a word from me, but you're not going to be able to find it or hear it. There will be nothing but uncertainty and confusion in your lives. You will run to and fro; you will run from the north to the south, the east to the west. There will be no word, no declaration from God of eternal truth. You have despised it, so I will remove it." There was a frantic search for truth.

"In that day" (v. 13), the day that God withholds his truth, his Word, there would be uncertainty because they would desperately need a Word from God and there would be none. God had spoken to them, but they had answered no. Have you ever wondered how Noah built the ark? I don't personally believe that he and his sons did all the work. I think there was too much to be done without help. Besides that how else would Noah have preached to the people? He preached for 120 years. The people heard the message and rejected it. They heard it, they listened. Noah preached, "Thus saith the Lord. Hear what God says.

Repent. Turn to God." But the thoughts and imaginations of mankind were nothing but evil continually, and men answered no to God.

One day God came down and said, "Noah, get into the ark with your family." And God shut the door, and I have an idea that if we ever do find Noah's ark, there will be grooves down the side of it where those who had rejected God tried to claw their way in when the water started to rise. There was no way in for them. They had rejected what they had despised. God withdrew from them.

I believe that we live in that kind of day. We have heard the gospel so much that it means nothing to us. We say that we believe, for instance, that all men without Christ are lost and are going to hell. Yet, how many of us have tried to win a soul? We don't really believe it. We have heard it all of our lives. We have said that Jesus Christ is our Lord and we live for his glory, but we are lazy. We are not disciplined. We are critical. We are not kind. We are contentious and rebellious, and all the time we are saying, "Jesus is my Lord." He is not. We have heard the gospel so much that we have become hardened. It has become commonplace.

We are exceedingly busy going through the motions of playing church. There is the deadly danger of being sidetracked. It can happen to all of us, whether convention presidents, pastors, laypersons, directors of denominational institutions, and others. We are so accustomed to doing what we call "spiritual things" that they have lost their sense of direction for us. We have taken hypocrisy and rebellion as such a norm for Christian experience that we don't even feel guilty anymore.

What would happen if God would withdraw what we have despised? What if God would take away what we have refused to hear? I have often wondered what would happen if God removed all the children that parents have used as excuses for not serving God. Or if God took our jobs and saw to it that they were no longer ours, if we have alibied that our jobs keep us from serving God. Or if God took the money we have hoarded and kept from God. I wonder what would happen if God would withdraw that which we despise as far as his glory is concerned. I personally believe that we are coming to that day. A day is coming when to be a Christian will require everything we are. Hypocrisy will be nigh onto impossible before much longer. There will be a culling out of those that do not mean business. A casual Christian will be an impossibility in a hostile world. God has allowed circumstances to enter our lives and our society where only the supernatural can deal with them. We can't handle it anymore. Be careful that we do not despise that which God has given us.

Notice two other ideas: When you reject truth it leaves an emptiness in your heart but it never stays empty. Error always bursts into the vacuum created by the absence of truth. Whenever we turn away from God's word, whenever we rebel against God, you can be sure that heresy will enter. False preaching will come in. The cults in our day are an example of this. Men who have rejected the truth of God now find themselves given over to man-made religions. The cults and the occult have in our day a growing patronage and constituency because people have rejected the truth. That was true in this passage. "They that swear by the sin of Samaria, and say, Thy God, O Dan, liveth." In Samaria and in Dan there was a corruption of the truth. There was a compromising, a mixture of the truth with pagan worship until the worship of God could scarcely be distinguished from paganism. When truth is rejected error fills the void.

Then what happens? Superstition gradually replaces spirituality. It says, "The manner of Beersheba liveth." That is rather obscure, but apparently great pilgrimages went to Beersheba. It was a long journey to Beersheba, and required discipline, and gradually people would comment, "If you were really spiritual you would go to Beersheba. It takes time, energy, effort, and inconvenience. The truly spiritual people make the journey to Beersheba. It didn't matter what happened when you arrived at Beersheba. Just the fact you went was important. In other words, putting out the effort to go there was seen as a reward in itself. That was nothing more than superstition.

We do the same thing, don't we? If you are spiritual, there are certain things you must do. I am not knocking that, but if you use those things to be spiritual, you're not spiritual. Our worship of God and our commitment to him ought to be compelled by the Holy Spirit because we love God and there is no other response. When I was ready to be married, nobody had to talk me into it. I wanted to do it. I was in love, and I wanted to marry Carol Ann. When you love God, and Jesus is the apple of your eye, you want to serve him. You want to please him and obey him. Your obedience and your service follow your love. Many people married out of a sense of duty and their marriages have been bad experiences. They have not been fulfillment and happiness because the end is not in the means.

Just going to Beersheba was not what God required. He did require a heart of love and devotion, and that applies to us. We have the idea that if we come to church we are spiritual. If you are a five-star Christian, you go Sunday morning, Sunday night, Wednesday night, and any other night they do anything at the church. Those are the five-star Christians. I happen to believe that a person sold out to Jesus will be active in every aspect of the church—but not in order to receive a grade from God. The Apostle Paul said, in essence, "I don't judge myself, and I don't care what anybody else thinks, because God judges me."

I wonder sometimes, *What are we doing?* Why do we come to church? We go away and think, *Boy, I didn't get anything out of that.* Why can't we get something out of worship? Maybe superstition has replaced spirituality, and we had thought that entering a church building somewhere would guarantee an encounter with God, yet without understanding what we needed to bring with us.

In Amos's day, they had rejected the truth. Error had filled the vacuum, and superstitions had replaced spirituality. There is a strong application for us today. The Bible has been given to us. Surely you have a Bible? Then prize it, share it, read it, study it, commit it to your heart. Do you attend a church where the pastor stands with a Bible in his hands and tries to preach the Word of God? Then hear it! Ask your friends to come hear it. Tell your community that your church has a man who is preaching the Word of God. Ask God to do something in his life and in that community. Pray for the preaching of the Word. You see, to possess a Bible and to hear the Word of God is not your inalienable right. You don't know that it will be your privilege indefinitely. Our compelling need is to hear what God has to say—and act upon it.

I believe that Satan has a real stronghold in our churches. We have been told we are spiritual so long that we have come to believe it. Indifference is a deadly stronghold in our church. Apathy is, too—we don't really care. We are not really concerned. There is no sense of expectancy in the service, no sense of God's moving in our hearts, no sense of urgency about our ministry. We have reasoned that indifference is not too bad and that it's not hostility. At least we're not against God—we're sort of treading water. Listen, indifference is open rebellion against God. Apathy is hostility towards God. You cannot remain neutral. The cross of Jesus Christ and the Word of God has made it impossible for anyone in any age to be a spectator. You cannot merely watch the drama of redemption and the panoramic ministry of the Word of God in the world. You are either working toward its fulfillment or against it. You cannot idly pass by the Word of God without someday having God withdraw that which you have despised.

If you drove out to the lake, and you were to see a child drowning, and you watched that child drown, you would be fully as guilty of that child's death as if you had pushed her in and held her under. Your indifference would have meant death. The same applies spiritually.

The people in Amos's day had come to a time when they despised the Word of God. God said, "OK, you don't want to hear me. I won't talk to you anymore. You don't want to obey me, so I will send you no more messages. You don't want to respond to my truth, so I'll take my word out of your midst." What they had despised, God withdrew. God is pleading with you. Whatever he wants you to do, do it (see John 2:5). If you don't, you are despising the Word of God. You are on shaky ground. In the Book of Revelation, Jesus is seen walking among the churches, and there is a golden candlestick which represents the privilege of hearing and proclaiming the Word—and ministering it. Jesus cautioned the churches that unless they were obedient and faithful, he would remove their candlesticks from their midst.

If we despise and bypass the Word of the Lord, he might well withdraw it. I do not want that to happen to us. God's Word must never be ignored, bypassed, or despised. If it is, God may withdraw the very truth we have despised. And that would be a tragedy of tragedies!

19
Inescapable Judgment
(Amos 9:1-10)

There is no escaping the major theme of Amos. The judgment of Almighty God against sin, whether corporate or individual, cannot be avoided. In these preceding chapters I have dealt in detail with the iniquities, transgressions, and sins of Israel as seen from the perspective of God whose spokesman was Amos.

What kind of profile could you write about the people of Israel? They were religious on the surface but not spiritual. Their forms and rituals were filled with play-acting and hypocrisy. They were haughty and discriminated against those who were less fortunate. They had "a form of godliness." They were a walking, talking contradiction. They went through all the motions of religious faith but, like the scribes and Pharisees of the New Testament, they left out the weightier matters—love, justice, and righteousness. They had shrouded their selfishness in religious terms.

In a word the Israelites were in a mess. Amos spared not. What else could he do? The message of God sizzled in his soul. The pyrotechnic power of God surged through his entire system. It was as if he had to unleash the message of God or explode.

In this passage there are five primary ideas. First, the coming judgment was *inevitable*. In 9:1 Amos wrote that he "saw the Lord standing upon the altar: . . . " God attended church that day. God wasn't standing by the altar. He was *on* it. It is certain that God's character will judge the nature of our worship. That has been true throughout Amos. Recall 4:2: "The Lord God hath sworn by his holiness." God was placing his own character on the line. And 8:6: "The Lord hath sworn by the excellency of Jacob." What a shock it would be if the Incarnate Lord bodily walked into our churches on Sunday morning! Yet, he's there all the time, and because we can't see him with the naked eye, we ignore the fact of his personal presence.

The acknowledged presence of the Lord should strip away the mask of hypocrisy. We can fool one another, but we can't deceive God. Anything contrary to his will is going to fall under judgment. Judgment now and later is an inevitability.

Second, the judgment was *inescapable*. "I will slay the last of them with the sword; he that fleeth of them shall not flee away, and he that escapeth of them shall not be delivered" (v. 1*b*). In other words, they would not get away. They would not escape. They would not be delivered.

What a chilling, blood-curdling message! "Though they dig into hell, thence shall mine hand take them; though they climb up to heaven, thence will I bring them down" (v. 2). On and on he continued with the theme that the Israelites could not escape judgment and punishment. He'd find them on the heights of Carmel. He'd locate them at the bottom of the sea. And it would be God's doing. "I will slay them." "I will bring them down." "I will take them out." "Thence will I command the serpent, and he shall bite them" (v. 3*b*). "I will set mine eyes upon them for evil" (v. 4*b*).

In Amos 5:18 were these unusual words: "Woe unto you that desire the day of the Lord!" Israel had the idea that when the day of the Lord came, God would punish all of Israel's enemies but leave Israel alone. For Israel the day of the Lord would be darkness and not light. Amos wanted to remind them that they were going to get their comeuppance. They weren't as privileged and exclusive as they thought.

Judgment was and is absolutely inescapable. One of Satan's subtlest tools is to give us the idea that we are exceptions to the rule. Think about the husband who says, "My wife doesn't understand me. She's cold toward me. We seldom have sex, so I'll find me a warm sex partner. God will understand." Don't count on it. Or the Christian who thinks he can cheat God and prosper in the long run. Or the teacher who accepts assignments to visit and never does. People naturally think that God is going to create a special dispensation for them.

This grievous fault expresses itself in many ways. First, we can become experts at what's wrong with everybody else. We never seem to understand that the faults we so readily see in others are probably our own faults as well. That's probably why we can ferret those sins out so well—we just can't see them in ourselves. Much is unsure today, but you can be certain of these things—God loves us but also that our sin will find us out. The wheels of God's judgment grind slowly, but they grind exceedingly fine.

If you waste an opportunity God has given you, you will live the remainder of your life under a cloud of that wasted opportunity. There was to be neither supernatural nor earthly refuge for Israel.

God even seems to hint, "If your enemies carry you away, and you are surrounded by their fortifications, I'll still use them to carry out my punitive will."

The third fact was: the judgment was *irresistible.* Here Amos took the concept of judgment and turned it back and forth. By this time I am sure the people either repented—and few of them did—or they were ready to kill Amos. You heard about the preacher who kept preaching on repentance. Finally, the deacons called him aside and asked, "What are you doing that for? There's no variety. You've preached on repentance until we're sick of it. When are you gonna quit it?" His answer: "When you folks repent." That reminds me of Amos.

Verse 5 refers to the truth that "the Lord God of hosts is he that toucheth the land, and it shall melt . . . and that all that dwell therein shall mourn: and it shall rise up wholly like a flood; and shall be drowned, as by the flood of Egypt." Amos justified his prophecy on the basis of the One who would carry out the judgment. "The Lord God of hosts." Amos has used that phrase repeatedly. It is perhaps the most superlative title that mankind could ascribe to God. It conveys awe and reverence in the presence of God's omnipotence and sovereignty. All he has to do is touch the earth and it melts. He moves in the floods.

Verse 6 refers to more of his power in nature. "It is he that buildeth his stories in the heaven, and hath founded his troop in the earth; he that calleth the waters of the sea, and poureth them out upon the face of the earth: The Lord is his name." The Lord—Jehovah, JHWH from the Hebrew tetragram—means the eternal I AM, the One who always was, who is, and who shall ever be. Devout Jews would not dare pronounce that name. When they reached that name in the reading of the Scriptures, they merely paused in hushed, reverential silence—then continued reading.

Isaiah 43 is also a breathtaking witness to the plentitude of God's graces and virtues. I wish it were possible for me to reproduce all of it here, but use your Bibles. Read the entire chapter with a receptive heart. It will transport you onto holy ground.

> Behold my servant, whom I uphold, mine elect, in whom my soul delighteth: I have put my spirit upon him: he shall bring forth judgment to the Gentiles. . . . But now thus saith the Lord that created thee, O Jacob, and he that formed thee, O Israel. Fear not: for I have redeemed thee. I have called thee by thy name: thou art mine. When thou passest through the waters, I will be with thee, and through the rivers, they shall not overflow thee; when thou walkest through the fire, thou shalt not be burned; neither shall the flame kindle upon thee. For I am the Lord thy God, the Holy One of Israel, thy Saviour; I gave Egypt for thy ransom, Ethiopia and Seba for thee. Since thou wast precious in my sight, thou hast been honourable, and I have

loved thee; therefore will I give men for thee, and people for thy life. Fear not: for I am with thee; . . . (Isa. 43:1-5a).

These promises are exquisite virtually beyond expression. Isn't that a glorious testimony of believers' relationships with Almighty God? Then, after twenty-one verses of God's supernatural and natural provisions for his people, the Scripture poignantly states: "But thou hast not called upon me, O Jacob (Israel); but thou hast been weary of me, O Israel." How hauntingly tragic. *But.*

Then God, through Amos, cataloged what the people had withheld from such a Provident God. Not only did they refuse to call on him, but they had greedily kept their sacrifices to themselves. The gist of this plaintive passage is—God had made no unreasonable, unfair demands on them. He never did and he never does. I am reminded of Paul's phrase in Romans 12:2— "which is your reasonable service."

"But thou hast made me to serve with thy sins, thou hast wearied me with thine iniquities" (v. 23*b*). The meaning of this strange verse is: "You have tried to dedicate your sins to me and you can't do it." God cannot bless sin. Sin is foreign to the nature of God. God cannot accept sin. Many times when we rededicate our lives, we are actually rededicating our sins. It won't work. It does no good to give God your sins unless you turn from them—if you don't leave them with God and let him handle your sins. What we do is make our own self-willed plans and then ask God to bless them. We are often apathetic, indifferent, and critical. Have you ever noticed that critical people are always contentious and unhappy? God protested about Israel, "You have made me to serve with thy sins."

In the remainder of Isaiah 43 God declared that Israel had profaned the princes of the sanctuary, had given Jacob to the curse, and Israel to reproaches. God had reemphasized that Israel stood in a unique position, but he would have to move against them because they did not honor the name which they bore. Judgment was irresistible.

Fourth, the judgment was *indiscriminate*. "Are ye not as children of the Ethiopians unto me? O children of Israel? Have not I brought up Israel out of the land of Egypt? and the Philistines from Caphtor, and the Syrians from Kir?" In other words, "What's the difference between you, Israel, and the heathen? Yes, I have chosen you but you have rejected my counsel. When it comes to judgment, you are no different." Through Amos, God had knocked in the head the mistaken notion that the Israelites could do what they pleased, and it was A-OK with God. They had presumed on God's goodness. They had taken him for granted, just like many of us today. "Surely God wouldn't send judgment on America, Christian America." Really? So-called Christian America in the last several decades has become a modern Babylon.

God showed Israel that its people were no different from the heathen, except they were more responsible because of their calling and their strategic position in God's plan for mankind. God was teaching them that, although they perhaps were not aware of their responsibility, they had always been accountable. In a sense all the nations of the world are the servants of God. For good or for ill, God still controls the ultimate destiny of the world. In reference to his people he was teaching, "I'm not looking at your historical past. I'm looking at your spiritual and moral present." He asked, "Where are you now? You're living in the past. You're tradition-bound." To couch it in Christian language, "Sure, you're saved. You can remember the time you committed your life to Christ. What does that mean to you today?" How does that affect your character, your life-style, your response today?

Verse 8 says, "Behold, the eyes of the Lord are upon the sinful kingdom, and I will destroy it from off the face of the earth; saving that I will not utterly destroy the house of Jacob, saith the

Lord." They looked back toward the Exodus, the Passover from Egypt. They were living in a dream world. They somehow thought that, regardless of what they did, the Exodus put God in debt to them. This passage was directed toward complacency which pretended godliness but only cared for itself.

That leads to the fifth thought—God's judgment is *incisive*. It is forceful and forthright. The truth is that God honors those who honor him. Yes, there were the faithful few. Doesn't most every church, no matter how bad off it is, have those loyal folks? Amos promises for God that the Lord would not completely destroy the house of Jacob. A remnant would be spared. The bulk of the populace would be carried away by the Assyrians. Verse 9 indicates that God would sift them. He would put them through trials and tribulations.

There will always be people in every generation who will love God with all their hearts. God always responds to such a people. Another truth is: There was an Israel within Israel. There was the bogus Israel and the genuine Israel. Note verse 10: "All the sinners of my people shall die by the sword, which say, The evil shall not overtake nor prevent us." The kind of sinner who is in the direst danger is the one who refuses to repent. He looks to the past and sees no need for alarm. He looks at the future and sees no judgment coming. "It couldn't happen here," he boasts. That's what Israel and Judah parroted. But it happened again and again. Sin. Captivity. Oppression. Slavery. Repentance of the remnant. Restoration. National sin. Captivity. . . . It was a vicious cycle throughout Hebrew history. That kind of sinner sees neither accountability nor responsibility.

Amos referred to sinners who think nothing of God's precepts or the grace by which they could be saved. They are insensitive, careless sinners living in a world of make-believe. They know all the right words. "I believe the Book. I believe in Jesus Christ. I adhere to the fundamentals of the faith." And that's marvelous. But they don't really believe with the heart. They see nothing in the nature of God which makes them responsible.

I think of the statement, "If the righteous scarcely be saved, where do the sinner and the ungodly appear?" If you're not real in your commitment to Christ, if you're faking it, you're facing the sword of judgment. You'll die innumerable deaths throughout eternity, but you will never cease to exist. Sin is suicide. Rebellion against God grinds the heart and life. If you are that kind of sinner you will die emotionally, mentally, physically, and spiritually.

But there is yet an invitation, in spite of your situation. Judgment is escapable only through Christ Jesus the Righteous. Flee to him!

20
God's Restoration
(Amos 9:11-15)

We have gone through about nine chapters of warning concerning judgment to come, nine chapters of deep castigation against the sins of Israel. Admit it or not we have seen ourselves reflected in many of these passages. In only a few years (722 BC) from Amos's message, the cruel Assyrians swooped down from the northeast and carried the Northern Kingdom into captivity. Ten of the tribes were deported, being separated from their kinsmen. To this day they are referred to as "the lost tribes of Israel."

The judgment God prophesied through Amos did fall. Now in this final chapter there is a change in mood and theme. Amos, in the Spirit, gazed into the future and envisioned the coming of the King, the Messiah, whose kingdom would be established— Jesus Christ who would consummate the final age as King of kings and Lord of lords. Amos, after heavy preaching on condemnation and judgment, now partly opened the curtains to let in the light of God's coming kingdom.

Remember that throughout Amos's scathing denunciations, there was always the call to repentance and the offer of God's grace. There was the reminder that God does respond to genuine prayer and to the pleas of those who love and serve him. In a real sense a forewarning of coming judgment was also a divine memo that the day of salvation would be in the offing. When God's judgment falls, when all wrongs are righted and brought under the scrutiny of a Holy God, salvation is also the

183

result. Amos longed for that kingdom which would cause future restoration.

The Apostle James almost eight centuries later, speaking at the Jerusalem Conference (Acts 15), quoted partly from Amos: "And to this agree the words of the prophets; as it is written, After this I will return, and will build again the tabernacle of David, which is fallen down; and I will build again the ruins thereof, and I will set it up: That the residue of men might seek after the Lord, and all the Gentiles, upon whom my name is called, saith the Lord, who doeth all these things" (vv. 15-17).

James harked back to this very passage in Amos 9. After punishment, trials, and destruction will come restoration. All that had kept devout followers of Jehovah going was hope of the restorative power of the Lord. Verse 11 here speaks of raising up "the tabernacle of David that is fallen," a rebuilding and restoration, "and close up the breaches [gaps and cracks] thereof; and I will raise up his ruins, and I will build it as in the days of old."

In a few translations the word *tabernacle* is rendered *booth*, the booth of David. Booth, even as it does today, seemed to mean a temporary place—flimsy and transitory. And no doubt the word booth would hint of the Feast of Booths (or Tabernacles). The feast was established when Israel had been nomadic people without a permanent home. The Feast of Tabernacles commemorated the people's leaving the wilderness and entering the Promised Land. As you know, Amos preached in the kingdom period when the nation was divided between the Northern Kingdom (Israel) and the Southern (Judah). One problem with which Amos grappled was the people's rebellion against the worship of Jehovah, egged on by wicked King Jeroboam I, one of the most ungodly monarchs in Israel's history. One of his first acts was to mock the Feast of Booths held in Judah. Jeroboam set up a false feast and mimicked the king of Judah and the high priest who would stand as a mediator between God and man.

Jeroboam had compromised the Feast of Booths.

Amos considered the feast and its corruption by a perverted king. He thought of the day when God would send a perfect royal Mediator, the real King. God would choose the "mediator between God and men, the man Christ Jesus" (1 Tim. 2:5). God's king would descend and sweep all enemies under his feet. What a ecstatic, holy thought. God is inexorably moving history toward its climax when the Lord will return and establish his kingdom upon the earth. "Jesus shall reign where'er the sun, Doth his successive journeys run, His kingdom spread from shore to shore, 'Til moons shall wax and wane no more." King Jesus will establish his kingdom and shall reign from a throne not made with human hands, but designed in the heart and mind of God.

Verse 12 carries with it the idea that sin's opposition to God will cease. "That they may possess the remnant of Edom, and of all the heathen, which are called by my name, saith the Lord that doeth this." This verse is resplendent with truth. "That they may possess the remnant of Edom." We need to understand that nearly every nation has had an antagonistic enemy. For Israel it had been Edom, its nearest neighbor. The people of Edom had betrayed Israel and through sabotage and subterfuge had opposed God and his people. Edom stood for the opposite of all that was godly and holy—the curse of sin, the power of evil against the purposes of God. When Amos spoke of Edom's overthrow, he was thinking of the complete crushing of all opposition to God. He envisioned a coming time when rebellion against God would no longer exist.

We are living in a hostile environment today, even as the Israelites were. All around us unsaved people want Christians to compromise their faith and join the crowd. In many public places you hear the charming name of Jesus only as an expletive. In essence, people are telling the Christians, as they told Amos, to "shut up."

Amos longed for the coming era when all opposition to God
and his purposes would be thwarted. This passage also alluded
to a new David who is going to come. Like the old David who
conquered and subdued Edom, the new David would conquer
and vanquish sin and its dread stranglehold.

But now look at this strange phrase: "And of all the heathen,
which are called by my name." How could the ungodly
Edomites be called by God's name? How could the heathen bear
his name. You have to realize that the concept of the kingdom
represented a universal kingdom to the Jewish writers. Amos
was emphasizing, "I see a time when even despised Edom and
the other heathen will be offered the salvation of God." Even
those heathen (the *goiim* to the Jews) would be included under
the name of God! The Jews were to be the conveyors of God's
redemptive purpose. Even the Gentiles would become heirs of
God and joint heirs with Christ Jesus. By faith the Gentiles who
embraced Jesus Christ would become spiritual sons of Abraham
and true Israelites!

The word *possess* suggested conquest. "Possess the land," the
Lord had instructed the Israelites concerning Canaan, meaning
take it, conquer it. This word also speaks of superior strength. In
ancient times when one nation conquered another, the conquered nation was called by the conqueror's name. In this case it
would have been Israel-Edom. The indication here is that any
land conquered by the Israelites would be called by God's name.
There is at least the inference here that once Israel conquered a
nation, that nation would be considered part of God's people.

Once a person has committed his life to God, there is an
equality of citizenship. The people of God are distinctive, yet
when we conquer for Christ we want the new members of God's
family to have all of God's privileges. There is no ranking system
in the kingdom of God. In God's mind we are all on an equal
plane. We are not called by the name of the church which
"conquered" or won us to the Lord. We are known by God's

name, signifying that all believers share a common heritage and inheritance. Human nature divides all of us into categories—black, white, red, yellow; fat, medium-sized, thin; North and South; East and West, "in" and "out," short and tall. But the gospel of redemption pulls all of us into one family of common origin with a common bond. What a miraculous picture of what happens when sin is conquered!

Verse 13 refers to the time when sin's curse will end. "Behold, the days come, saith the Lord, that the plowman shall overtake the reaper, and the treader of grapes him that soweth seed; and the mountains shall drop sweet wine, and all the hills shall melt." That is a picture which should delight every farmer, a portrayal of lavish and spontaneous abundance. The verse speaks of crops so lavish that those harvesting the crop will overrun those planting the next crop. "The mountains shall drop sweet wine, and all the hills shall melt" is another description of fruitfulness and overflowing abundance. This verse reminds you of a sweetness "that melts in your mouth." Here Amos is looking toward the millennial kingdom, a time of unprecedented abundance.

The world as we know it is benighted with the curse of sin. It is a world devastated by natural disasters—earthquakes, tidal waves, typhoons, tornados, volcanic eruptions, blizzards, and heatwaves. We know of the blistering sun that withers and kills and the torrential rains and floods which sweep everything away in their paths. It is an earth of snakes and vipers, poisonous spiders, destructive animal and insect pests, thorns and thistles, diseases and blights. Mankind and his world have laid under the curse since the Fall in the Garden of Eden.

But, praise the Lord, Amos foretells the golden day when sin's curse will have ended. I have already mentioned Paul's statement that all of the creation groaneth and travaileth for the second coming of the Lord Jesus Christ. Even nature cries out for restitution. And every person does the same deep down inside, whether or not he receives the Redeemer. When Jesus establishes his kingdom, all of us will be delivered from the bondage of corruption. All of creation will be liberated. The curse will be gone and Eden will be reinstated. Can you see that? All these years the earth has been bound. But in the kingdom bondage is removed. The sun will never shine a second too long, only enough to give light and sustenance to the earth. It will never rain a drop too many. No need for water sprinklers or fertilizer. The earth will be in a perfect condition as it yields bumper crops and lays its bounty at the feet of the only King who has the right to reign over nature.

Verse 14 tells us that sin's power will be destroyed. The people accepted the harvest found in verse 13 and were blessed by it. Verse 14 says: "I will bring again the captivity of my people of Israel, and they shall build the waste cities, and inhabit them; and they shall plant vineyards, and drink the wine thereof; they shall also make gardens, and eat the fruit of them."

What a contrast this is to Amos 5:11 which emphasized, "Ye have built houses of hewn stone, but ye shall not dwell in them; Ye have planted pleasant vineyards, but ye shall not drink wine of them." Then there was the statement in 5:12: "For I know your manifold transgressions, and your mighty sins." In chapter 5 the observation was made that the people had set out to find security, satisfaction, "the good life." But they were frustrated in their desires because when people live in rebellion toward God, nothing can ensue but disappointment and waste. That's always the pattern. When we rebel against God, we hurt ourselves. We bring anguish and despair upon ourselves. They struggled for pleasure and satisfaction, but it turned into the winepress of the wrath of God. But in God's kingdom Amos 5:11-12 will be reversed. God's people will eat the fruit of their gardens. Sin will no longer blight. They will live comfortably in the houses they build. Only in God can we have a sense of security and satisfaction.

You cannot find peace in financial security. Finances are wobbly as I write these words. We are not far removed from another Great Depression. Many who read this book have no recollection of the Great Depression. Even now the unemployment rate lacks only a few percentage points being what it was in the depths of the Depression. We dare not trust in mammon and materialism.

Amos 9:15 goes: "And I will plant them upon the land, and they shall no more be pulled up out of their land which I have given them, saith the Lord thy God." That verse promises us that sin's penalty will be removed. Throughout the Old Testament, if the people went away from God, if they rebelled against him, they could lose their inheritance. It was a conditional covenant. Here is the plain promise that they would never "be pulled up out of their land." If the land is theirs forever, they cannot lose it. This spoke of the age when sin would no more abound and reign. It meant that the penalty of sin had been removed, and they would never again feel its burdensome weight.

Amos viewed a new society under the King, a civilization where sin's rule had collapsed, where there was no hostility to the will of God. He foresaw an earth which yielded in unimpeded abundance, where the people lived in security and deepdown satisfaction. A kingdom was coming where sin's penalty had been removed and where God's pledge would be their's forever. God promised that kind of kingdom. God cannot by his nature deceive or lie, and he promised that such a kingdom was coming. Jesus taught us to lift up our heads, "for your redemption draweth nigh."

"The kingdom is coming, O tell ye the story, God's banner exalted shall be, The earth shall be full of his knowledge and glory like waters that cover the sea." But we can have a foretaste of that blessed kingdom right now. When we respond to Christ, we don't have to wait for that kingdom. The seeds of that kingdom are planted in our hearts when we bow to him in faith and obedience. That King comes to reign and rule within our hearts, and when he does, everything that Jesus is, he is in us! He is the King of kings ruling within us. All of us long for that security and satisfaction—and it is found only in him. He will not force his reign upon you. He desires willing subjects. He will be Lord in you when you allow him to be.

"Seek the Lord, and ye shall live; . . . " (5:6).